Geri o Shimasu

Adventures of a Baka Gaijin

BY ALIA LURIA

Geri o Shimasu: Adventures of a Baka Gaijin
Copyright © 2025 Alia Luria
All Rights Reserved.
Published by Unsolicited Press.
Printed in the United States of America.
First Edition.

No part of this book may be used or reproduced in any manner whatsoever without written permission except in the case of brief quotations embodied in critical articles or reviews. People, places, and notions in this book are from the author's imagination or memory; any resemblance to real persons or events is purely coincidental.

Attention schools and businesses: for discounted copies on large orders, please contact the publisher directly.

For information contact:
Unsolicited Press
Portland, Oregon
www.unsolicitedpress.com
orders@unsolicitedpress.com
619-354-8005

Cover Design: Kathryn Gerhardt
Editor: S. Stewart
ISBN: 978-1-963115-54-3

To Vince-
I can't wait to experience
Japan through your eyes.

CONTENTS

From the Author	9
Geri o Shimasu!	16
Ainote	26
The Togoshi Ginza Ripper	29
Ainote	38
Salsa on Home	40
Ainote	49
No Time for Love, Doctor Jones!	52
Ainote	62
That Time the Train Was Delayed	64
Ainote	77
Don't Bother with Translation	81
Ainote	90
A Labia-Scalding Night on the Town	93
Ainote	105
Yakuza-a-Go-Go	108
Ainote	119
I Was a Day-Old Christmas Cake	121
Ainote	132
No Soup for You!	134

Ainote	143
Mind the Gap	145
Ainote	154
I Skull Fuck… and Other Engrish Atrocities	156
Ainote	165
Kanamara Matsuri: The Festival of the Steel Phallus	168
Ainote	175
Roppongi Redux	177
Ainote	183
All Good Things Must Come to an End…	185

Geri o Shimasu
Adventures of a Baka Gaijin

FROM THE AUTHOR

2008 was a year of expansion. Packing a giant suitcase and moving to a foreign country with a 14-hour time difference from my friends and family in a time before Google maps and translation apps where the language, culture, and even writing system are vastly different from my own forced me to adapt in ways I'd never had to before. The experience uncurled pieces of me knotted so tight I didn't realize they were there. I was vulnerable in a way that I'd never been vulnerable before, and it was freeing. Living as an outsider allowed me to observe my surroundings from a lens of complete detachment free from any social expectation, while still appreciating the value of my own culture. I made mistakes, sometimes incredibly embarrassing ones. I made friends, some of whom I still consider friends fifteen years later. I made decisions about the person I wanted to be, and those decisions shaped who I became. They also shaped how I want to live and helped me crystallize my priorities.

Conversely, the year 2017 was, in total, the worst year of my life for a plethora of reasons that require an entirely separate volume outside of the scope of these essays. I was forced to look inward to tackle a lot of negative experiences, both personally and professionally, romantically, and family-related, my physical vulnerability as a woman, and even the fundamental trust that I thought I had in people who were supposed to be friends. This experience has shaped the years since, making me prioritize my own needs in my personal and professional lives. That reactionary correction shaped how I choose to live, has been amazing for my professional career, and has truly made me happy with myself, my life, and my chosen path.

The flip side is that my experiences in 2017 hardened me. I'm just as blunt and open with who I am, but I tend to close myself off to new feelings I would have embraced before 2017. People I love and trust are cherished in my life, but the circle doesn't grow easily, especially with romantic partners. This reality makes me even more grateful for those people in my life who have contributed to my well-being and who have allowed me to contribute to theirs, but it does have an impact, one I am still working through and processing.

And this experience, now, in 2023, of writing about that time in 2008 through the lens of who I've become since 2017, gives me the mental space to revisit my trials, triumphs, and massive fails and reminds me that vulnerability is the necessary first step towards intense growth. Maybe I'll never be as open as I was in 2008 living the *baka gaijin* (stupid foreigner) life in Tokyo, but there is a middle ground between embracing the radical vulnerability of living out of my depth in every respect and closing myself off to emotional growth in a frankly vain effort to protect myself from hurt.

These essays are presented in rough chronological order from the time I arrived until the time I departed Japan, but you will note that they sometimes skip around in time within the story. I try to let the theme ground events revealed. Like this introduction, they might jump around and interrupt themselves. I hope they convey the movement of memory and thought and the fragility of perception. Also, I think that part of appreciating the immersion into another culture is the context that comes with facts and explanations, but I didn't want to weigh down the narrative flow. Sorry in advance for all the footnotes, but their digressions and whimsy add both the necessary context as well as additional color to the immersive experience.

I invite you now to explore with me a time in my life where uncertainty was the only constant and life was magical in its absurdity. Also, there are poop jokes!

A Note on Schadenfreude: Schadenfreude is an interesting emotion. Having been observed in children as young as 24 months, it is a reflexive human reaction to revel in the misfortune of others. A feeling of instant joy with no real benefit to our psyche. In fact, research published in New Ideas in Psychology indicates that schadenfreude is linked to aggression and rivalry and has a negative relationship with self-esteem. It makes us feel better in the short term to celebrate the misfortunes of others, but in the end, your misery does not make my life better, and my misery does not make your life better. The joy is fleeting, and the result is inconsequential. But…in the interest of enjoying this book, and laughing at my misadventures, please embrace your feelings of schadenfreude. You have my permission to giggle when you think about my poor outcomes. Please chortle when I suffer embarrassment. I do! And that's because these experiences while replete with misfortune were an amazing time in my life, and there is nothing emotionally vacuous about sharing them with you, vomit, injury, and sharp edges included.

A note on *haiku* (or *senryu* for the observant): I will be the first to assure you that I am not a poet. I very occasionally turn to the form in times of great emotional distress when my thoughts won't come to me any other way. Of the few non-*haiku* poems that I've written over the years, the first, penned about my strained relationship with my father during my parents' divorce, was to be included in a middle school literary magazine, but the only hand-written copy was sadly lost by my teacher prior to its publication, gone forever.

I remember being made to read it to my Language Arts class, and a boy in the class saying, "Is that about her boyfriend?" It's worth noting I was both twelve and a nerd.

"It's about her father," my teacher snapped in response, and though my face flamed, the floor did not reach up to swallow me whole. In retrospect, I'm probably not sad that this foray failed to solidify my journey towards poetry.

The second poem was written about a boyfriend that I had from college through my mid-twenties. I wrote it for myself in a notebook by our bed in all that early twenty-something angst and frustration. It disappeared at some point between one apartment and the next, and I only learned years after we parted that he had found it and taken it for himself. He's a bit of a hoarder, so he probably still has it. Again, I have no other record of it.

The last few poems were written in 2017 as I was going through the hell-year described above; a couple were about a lost friendship and my frustration at the inability to communicate with the person, and one was about my friend Heather that I haven't tried to get published anywhere, because it's for me and reminds me of the joy she brings me. In short, my attempts at any formal poetry are largely not meant to be seen by the masses. The closest brush was a piece "Paralysis" published in the now defunct (thanks to COVID) but lovely *Toho Journal*, which could either be described as prose poetry or flash fiction depending on who you ask.

That preface aside, I have always felt the quiet magic of *haiku*, my appreciation for the form existing well before my time in Japan. They were the first poetry drafting we learned in school, and in 2017, I turned to composing them in my head while I was stressed out as a simple form of meditation. When my mind was caught in a feedback loop, taking the focus to develop a syllabically and thematically accurate *haiku* helped my mind reset. It doesn't hurt that jotting them down on a phone is easy as well. As time progressed, I found that *haiku* was another form of journaling for me, and it has become an immensely satisfying part of my writing practice.

In a similar vein, the inimitable Jack Kerouac scribbled over 1,000 haikus in notebooks, woven into his prose, and eventually compiled into a tome of them, which was not published until after his passing.[1] It is titled *Book of Haikus* and contains 500 of the tiny vignettes. Kerouac abandoned the strict Japanese syllabic requirements (called the *on*) in composing his poems, choosing instead to focus on the economy of language, *kireji* (cutting word), and *kigo* (seasonality) that are the essence and thematic guides to composing *haiku*.[2] His goal, and one I share with him as an avid

---

[1] See, this is what I mean by digressions. Kerouac mainly worked in a term that he called American Pops, or American Haikus. The use of an "s" to pluralize *haiku* is something unique to Kerouac, since most of us just use the word *haiku* to reference both the singular and plural of the form. He changed the name of the form from *haiku* to pops to express that his poetic form was an adaptation, not an adherence. It was a redefinition of the genre, one for which is he known in literary circles.

[2] As an aside, *senryu* is a form similar to *haiku* but which forgoes the *kigo*. Any discussion of *on*, *kireji*, and *kigo* is loose at best, as the structure of the Japanese language (which follows the word order subject object verb rather than English's subject verb object structure) and nuanced differences

composer of *haiku*, is to tell a complete story or paint a whole picture in three simple lines.

During his life, Kerouac spent decades mastering the spirit of *haiku*, so if you want a better example than me of American Pops, please check out his book. For me, given my history with the Japanese language and sentence structure, I find the mental work of observing the seventeen *on* (phonetic unit) requirement of *haiku* as such would be composed in Japanese assists in the therapeutic nature of the form. Maybe one day I will ascend to the levels of Kerouac and let the *on* fall away leaving only the *kireji* and *kigo* to guide me, but I am not there yet. So, please enjoy my collection of *haiku* interspersed through these stories. Traditionally grouped by either season or theme, I have grouped mine by thematic content (such as growth, loss, anxiety, etc.) paired with an ink and watercolor drawing done from photographs I took during my adventures.

A note on *ainote*: *Ainote* is a Japanese word that can be translated as interlude, in a musical sense, but can also be used to describe either a rhythmic clapping or chanting that accompanies a song, or an interjection or interruption. With respect to my *haiku* sections, I title each of them as *ainote*. I chose this use of the word for

---

in words mean that English has no literal equivalent to any of these Japanese terms. Having studied the Japanese language both formally and independently, though I am not expert at its many complexities, has given me a sense of cadence in my own composition of *haiku* that I think makes the form more natural to me. Also, that Japanese is naturally formatted such that the subject is first disclosed, then the object, and finally the verb adds to the sense that a complete story is possible in the composition of every sentence. There is a natural tension to how information is revealed to the listener.

interlude because I wanted to evoke the musicality and lyrical qualities of *haiku* but to also create a pause or break in the narrative structure. Whether my *haiku* are a mental break from the stories or whether the stories are a break from the *haiku*, I guess I don't know. That's for the reader to decide.

GERI O SHIMASU!

As a second-year law student at the ripe old age of thirty, I was extremely excited to spend an entire semester living in Tokyo. To see the sites, practice my Japanese, and study international law was living the dream. I had made it through the grueling first year of law school, survived on-campus interviews in the first half of the second year, managed to keep my GPA up, and even secured a summer associate position for the summer of 2008 with an AMLAW 100 law firm. It was now January 2008, and I was ecstatic to have five months to live in Japan and absorb its culture, food, and sites.

However, I wasn't even there twelve hours when the country asserted my status as a *gaijin*, the Japanese word for foreigner. I had a kidney infection in the December leading up to the beginning of the semester and was required to make the trip there while still on what I can only describe as an ass-load of antibiotics. In an attempt to beat the infection, which had been lingering, I had been on a cocktail of three separate heavy-duty antibiotics for a number of weeks prior to my arrival. In my excitement to be starting my study abroad adventure, one that I had been planning since before I even applied to law school, I gave little thought to the status of my kidneys or my gut, which apparently did not take well to being stripped of its natural fauna and promptly sent off to a new country to recover.

Let's back up a moment. Upon my arrival, my school arranged for temporary lodging in a Japanese-style hotel to incoming students. We were able to book a room at a small local hotel near our campus for up to two weeks at the beginning of the term. Because we were each tasked with securing our own housing during the program, this was designed to ease the transition for students and allow us a little breathing room to find apartments in Tokyo. With respect to the hotel, Japanese-style meant that, among other things, there was one communal, multi-stall restroom for the whole floor and a tiny room for individuals to sleep in, each one housing a twin bed. Under most circumstances, I really love immersing myself in a culture. As a welcome to Japan, my school treated us to a truly excellent dinner. And. I. Ate. All. The. Things. Including the *sashimi*, the *shabu shabu*, and anything that came across my plate.[1] It was all great... until I woke up in the middle of the night literally having shat my pajamas in my sleep. And it wasn't the well-formed, intact kind, if you know what I mean.

Oh, the horror! The only thing worse than waking up in your own diarrhea is knowing that you need to get yourself physically down a hallway, into a communal restroom and not be spotted by anyone else while waddling and smelling like... honestly, I have no words about the smell.

Why didn't you just change in your room? you ask.

Well, I just didn't have the necessary supplies to clean up that kind of biohazard scene, and I'll leave it at that. After somehow creeping down the hall, making it to the bathroom, cleaning myself

---

[1] See the essay "Don't Bother with Translation" for a detailed description of *shabu shabu*.

up as I cursed my own body and my life while listening to the happy toilet music (because Japan), I managed to get back into my room and fall back asleep. Until I woke up again and... yes... I shat myself again. It was probably one of the worst nights of my life. Plus, I was down two sets of flannel pajama bottoms and I'd only been in the country fourteen hours. I think you see where I'm going with this.

I figured that this situation would run its course, pun intended, but things did not improve. It was like my body was not just rejecting the food but my very organs. Finally, when the need to rush to the bathroom subsided for more than ten-minute increments, I called my mother over Skype to ask what to do. She's a physician, and for that, I was and am still very, very lucky.

She explained to me the names of the medications I would need. I had one more request, however. Could she look up the Japanese word for diarrhea for me? In case you ever need this information, the word is *geri*.

Normally, I would have crawled back into bed and dealt with the admin side of life later, but I had another pressing matter. Given the obscenely complicated requirements and customary payments required to lease an apartment in Japan, I opted for one of the no fuss guesthouses that are very popular.[2] They are an excellent

---

[2] My guesthouse was operated by a company called Sakura House if you are looking for a place to live in Tokyo without dealing with the convoluted Japanese rental requirements, including deposits and key money, or *reikin* (literally "gratitude money"). Key money is a mandatory payment, usually a doubling of the rental deposit to up to three months of rent. It varies, though, and can actually be up to six or more months of rent, which you can see would make it extremely difficult for a student to afford, particularly one only staying in Japan for five months total. Key money requirements have slowly changed over the years, and some landlords forgo it as an enticement for renters, but in 2008, it was alive and well and extremely burdensome! As to

housing option for *gaijin*, except when said *gaijin* is required to travel half-way across a city of thirty-six million people to collect the key to said guesthouse and make this trip within forty-eight hours of a projected move-in date, twenty-four of which had already been spent donating her intestines to the Japanese sewer system.

I gathered my cramping body, a paper map printed from MapQuest[3], my non-working original iPhone,[4] my cash, and my hotel key (yes, a physical key) and did what any sane person presented with my facts would do... get into an exceptionally expensive cab and make the driver deal with getting me to the guesthouse office. Japanese cabs really are amazing, but they make you pay for this extreme convenience, and there's no 'I'm a foreign

---

guesthouses, they do charge a small deposit but never charge key money, and contracts are extremely flexible. Sakura House is still in business today and has actually grown even larger. They have properties all over Tokyo, and you can rent flexibly for as long as you plan to stay. If you're looking for a reputable option, I highly recommend them.

[3] Kids, ask your parents what this is. Actually... if you don't remember MapQuest, are you even old enough to be reading this?

[4] Note that in 2008, Japan didn't receive coverage for the iPhone until June 9. I left Japan in late May. I actually had the original iPhone, a Christmas present in 2007, but, at the time, it was AT&T-only, and it wasn't compatible with Japanese cellular providers were I to find a way to unlock it. Also, as an American, I would most likely have had to buy a Japanese phone and then put the Japanese sim into my American phone, because most cellular providers wouldn't sell you a SIM for a phone not available in Japan. At the time, you could not even purchase a cell phone until you had your Japanese ID card, and having just arrived, I did not yet have that either. Needless to say, I was SOL on cell service for a couple weeks. I used my laptop and Wi-Fi to Skype my friends and family back home.

student dying of intestinal distress discount."[5] The cab dropped me right at a relatively squat building in the middle of a busy street in

---

[5] Generally, I reserved taxis for an "emergency" situation, e.g., where I was lost and pressed for time. For instance, on my first day of class, I somehow got lost between the Asakusa train station and the Temple University Japan law school campus. Don't ask me how, as the walk between the train station and my classes was maybe seven minutes. Desperate and late, I flagged a Japanese taxi. Even in 2008, every taxi came equipped with GPS, except, of course, the one I happened to get into that day when I was lost. Normally, I would just read off the address of where I was going, and the taxi driver would enter it into his GPS and off we'd go. The reason why GPS is so critical in Japan is because the postal address convention is completely and utterly insane. I don't criticize a country's bureaucracy lightly, but for some crazy ass reason, addresses in Japan are not linear down a street. They are by zone, each zone being a square area of the city, and building numbers are assigned chronologically based on when in time the building was built. So, you could be driving down a street and every building is a random number. You cannot "feel your way" around Tokyo when you need to get to a specific building. I honestly don't know how anyone found anything before GPS, but there were a lot of hand-drawn maps. So, I get into this cab, and start to rattle off the address, and the driver, wearing his little white gloves and jaunty hat, pulls out an ancient paper atlas, and my heart squeezes in my chest. Half the pages are falling out, and I look on in horror as he begins to leaf through it, searching for the specific zone of my address.

"*Mō ichido onegaishimasu,*" he asked (Please say it again)

"*Ni, hachi, jū-ni, Minato-ku,*" I repeated haltingly, forgetting to include the particle *no* between my numbers. (2-8-12 Minato) In 2017, TUJ moved to Setagaya, but at the time, the campus was still in Minato.

"Ah," he said, taking a moment to parse my response, and continues to leaf around.

I peered over the seat as he bent his head close to the tiny book muttering to himself and trying to read by a streetlight, as the sun had already set. My class had started by this point, but I endeavored not to take my stress out on him. He found the *chome* (zone), which was 2, and then started digging through the following pages for the block and building, 8-12. He tried to involve me in this process, speaking quickly and pointing at parts of the map, and I scanned the page with him looking for the numbers. Mercifully, numbers are Romanized in addresses. It was a tense number of minutes before he finally exclaimed and pointed, showing me the referenced portion of the map. Relief immediately washed through me. I was now a good thirty minutes late to class.

"*Mita ka?*" he asked. (See that) "*Kore ga.*" (There it is)

He said more, but I couldn't understand. Most likely, he was explaining how he'd managed to find the address or telling me something about how it was very hidden. I squinted at the tiny numerals.

"*Hai,*" I replied enthusiastically, trying to show my appreciation through my limited communication. "*Arigatou gozaimasu.*" (Yes, thank you very much)

Consensus reached, he pulled into traffic and we proceeded along the route set out in the paper map. Perhaps ten minutes later, we were driving down a side road looking for the building. In Japan, if one person commits to helping another person, they do not half ass it. They are honor bound to follow their assistance through to a final resolution. It was no different for the taxi driver. We scoured the street for the building number, and I was starting to panic that this poor driver and I were going to grow old together. My new life as a ward of the Tokyo taxi company was about to begin when I recognized the door to the campus.

"There," I yelled in English, too excited to try to remember my Japanese. "It's there." He stopped quickly and looked dubiously between the map and the door.

"OK *desu*," I improvised, smiling to show that we had found it. (It is OK)

"OK," he repeated, still not quite convinced, and I paid for the ride in cash. In Japan, you don't open the door of a taxi. There's a lever where the driver sits, and he opens and closes the door with this lever, so I had to wait for him to release me from the cab, which he finally did, nodding a bow.

Shinjuku. The sheer size of the city around me was boggling. Sorry, New York, home of my birth, but you've got nothing on Tokyo. It is hard to understand the scale of Tokyo from photos. The buildings are taller and denser than you think, the streets wider than you expect, and the people more numerous than you can imagine. Still trying to catch my breath from being smack in the middle of it all, I climbed the stairs to the registration office, pale as a ghost and trying not to think of the massive throng of strangers into which I had dropped myself.

As is the nature of accomplishing anything in Japan, I completed the ridiculous amount of paperwork involved in renting a room. I had already pre-booked it online, but this did not actually reduce the amount of paperwork, which was mercifully in English due to the fact that guesthouses cater to foreigners. I was required to complete all paperwork in person at the office, and they helpfully had some desks set aside for those of us slogging through it all in hopes of getting a key to an apartment some time before we died of old age. The Japanese love of bureaucracy truly befuddles me, and I'm a lawyer, so that's saying something. I thanked whatever Shinto gods kept me from having another intestinal episode while I was waiting and stepped, finally, with guesthouse key in hand, back into the crazy, busy streets of a completely foreign city to which I had barely seen let alone acclimated. I looked around me trying to get my bearings and spotted what looked like a convenience store across the narrow block. Score! It was a pharmacy.

"*Arigato gozaimashita,*" I repeated and bowed to him before dashing into the building and to my class, which was almost over by the time I took my seat. After that I memorized the path from the school to the train very carefully. (Thank you for what you did)

I attempted to enter through the pharmacy's sliding doors only to find that sliding doors in Japan are not automatic. They are operated by touching a panel where the two doors meet in the center. Slamming my face into the door as I tried to enter didn't help the Japanese perception of me or my skull. After some searching, I successfully found the button to push to activate the door.[6] Inside was a diminutive man in slacks and a button down with round glasses. He was organizing the shelves with a solemn expression on his face, and I could see that he worked there.

"*Sumimasen,*" I said. (Excuse me)

"*Hai*", he said. (Yes)

"*Geri o shimasu,*" I said. (I translate this as I have diarrhea, but literally it means I do diarrhea, which I'm sure only added to the horror for this pharmacy clerk)

"*Oh... so desu ne?*" he asked. (Oh... is that so)

His face registered no change of expression at all, but I knew enough about Japanese people from language lessons and cultural studies to know that this was a socially ingrained reaction to someone sharing something completely inappropriate with them. He really, really wished I hadn't said what I had said.

"*Hai,*" I replied. Nothing like doubling down on the awkwardness. (Yes or, technically, that's correct)

---

[6] It was common for pre-COVID Japan to have doors that open on touch rather than automatically, but I have read that they made changes to their doors to no longer require touching them after COVID. I believe the impetus for having doors that needed to be touched kept doors from opening constantly as people walked by. As crowded as Tokyo is, this makes sense. It wastes energy to have doors constantly opening as people crowd the outside streets.

Look, I spoke some Japanese, but at that point it was relatively limited. This was the first conversation I ever had in Japanese with a Japanese person in Japan, cab driver notwithstanding. The cab driver mostly communicated with smiles and bows. Needless to say, this was probably the most mortifying conversation that either of us had ever had, and I had just walked into a glass door, so I wasn't starting from a position of confidence. I suspect that clerk still remembers me about as fondly as I remember that day.

After digesting my announcement for a moment, he silently led me to a section of the pharmacy and gestured with spread hands to a shelf of medication near the ground. I tried to ask him which one, but he just gestured insistently, not meeting my eyes and then backed away, leaving me to sort out the options myself. None of the active ingredients of the indicated medications matched the names my mom had given me. I should probably have considered myself lucky that they were even in Roman letters and readable. It was such a good day. Not wanting to risk guessing incorrectly, I just picked up one of everything and took it to the counter where the clerk rang up my purchases completely silently. I couldn't tell if he was embarrassed for me or scared of me. Either way, the silence followed me all the way to the street. I'm sure he was glad to see me go. At least I managed not to walk square into the door on the way out.

From there, I suffered a super uncomfortable series of train rides back to my hotel. This was my first ride on the Japanese train system, which I really, really love. It's clean as a whistle, always on time, and gets you almost everywhere you need to go in Tokyo. At this early point in my relationship with the trains, however, I spent my time praying silently to myself that I was on the right train headed in the right direction and would somehow be able to find my way back to my hotel room in Mita. I didn't really have the cash for another cab ride. The cramps came and went, but the Shinto gods spared me and the other passengers on the Ōedo Line from another pants-staining. The train and a fifteen-minute walk later, I called my mom again and cursed the fourteen-hour time difference. She got onto the computer and looked up all the names I read her until we sorted out what I had brought and at what quantity. She marveled that anyone saw relief at all from the dosages, a common theme in Japan, where even antibiotics are dosed low, sometimes requiring multiple doctor visits. As an example, my friend Becky, after the same welcome dinner, ended up with a bacterial infection that required multiple rounds of antibiotics to resolve, because the initial dosages prescribed weren't therapeutic by American standards.[7]

"Just take three now, and then take another one every time you feel the urge," she said. "Even if it's right after. Take them until it stops."

Like a good thirty-year-old girl suddenly living in another country with literally no clue what to do next, I listened to my mommy and popped anti-diarrheal tablets like candy. Even with the pitifully weak medication, it did eventually (not for a while) stop. And I did move into my new-to-me guesthouse apartment half-way across the city in a third direction from both the leasing office and my hotel.

Even today, the happy toilet music still haunts me mockingly.

---

[7] See the story "Yakuza a Go-Go" for more about Becky's experience.

AINOTE

I made this ink and watercolor sketch from a photograph that I took of the Japanese cemetery, Higashi Otani, in Kyoto, Japan, March 2008 during my Spring Break visit

>Golden light—distilled
>through flesh, bone, and to the soil—
>day fading slowly.

And in that instant,
frozen frame of cold, harsh light—
for you, it ended.

And yet I don't weep
for friends lost to the ages,
for they were not mine.

Tiny bones rattle—
pieces of you here with me
now until the end.

Clear and cold and bright,
frozen crystals exhale but
my voice cracks silent.

Rain beats down then boom;
thunder splits the quiet night,
but my house still stands.

Snuffed in an instant—

fragile life slipping away
and so, cut too short.
Tip tap of the foot;
snap crack of the knuckle bone;
blink twitch of the eye.

The words felt heavy
in her hand, like a raised knife—
crackling with rage.

THE TOGOSHI GINZA RIPPER

My home base in Tokyo was the little area of Togoshi in the Shinagawa Ward. Tokyo is so large that it's more like a giant ring of areas none of which are really suburbs, as we might define such in the United States. At the time, Temple University Japan was located in one of the areas along the edge of the ring formed by the Yamanote train line that circles the city. Mita was the area where campus was located, and this is a foreigner-heavy business district in central Tokyo. It wasn't super residential, so most of the students in my class scattered to the winds, ending up in areas around this central district. I had friends all over, including Shinjuku, Gotanda, Asakusa, Ueno, and some, like myself, living in Togoshi.

    I lived on the fourth floor of a seven-story building. Each floor starting with the second floor was a single guesthouse apartment rented by the room and shared among two to three people. The first floor was this tiny Nepalese restaurant with the best food ever. When I say tiny, I mean it had a counter that sat like two people and one table that also sat two people. A large portion of the actual space in the restaurant was dedicated to the diminutive kitchen that housed a massive tandoori oven which was clearly visible to patrons and provided a superior olfactory experience. There was many an evening where I had every intention of eating the groceries sitting in my refrigerator, but the smell of that restaurant would change my mind before I even made it to the elevator.

My particular room was unique in the building because I opted for a Japanese style room with a *tatami* (woven hemp mat) floor and *shoji* (wooden frame with translucent paper panels) that served as the door to my room. I actually chose this particular location because of this room, and it was a fairly reasonable ¥96,000 ($960) per month. My bed was a *futon* (a quilted cotton mattress) on the floor. Most of the rooms in the building, including the other two rooms in my apartment were done in the western style with wood floors and bed frames supporting spring mattresses. Traditional Japanese rooms are measured in the number of *tatami* mats it takes to cover the floor. My room was small by American standards but was big enough by Japanese standards to have slept a whole family. The room itself was more than fifty percent larger than the other two bedrooms in my apartment. My room also had a sliding window that opened to a patio, where I could stand outside and look over Togoshi Ginza.

When I first arrived at my apartment and was still on good terms with my Australian roommate, he showed me around and explained the kitchen and washer to me. The washing machine was a combination washer/dryer, and because it wasn't very good at drying, he told me I would probably want to let it run for a bit but then ultimately hang my clothes on my patio to dry. We went out to the patio to look around.

"Don't leave your panties here to dry overnight, though," he said after a moment, his face serious.

"I'm sorry," I said. I had just met this man, and now he was talking about my underwear. *Also, was there some rule against underpants being publicly displayed after dark that I wasn't aware of?*

30

"Most laundry is fine," he clarified, "but if you leave your underwear here, it will be stolen."

"We are four floors up," I said and snuck a peek over the edge of the concrete wall of the patio.

He reached up his arm and smacked the wall to the right side of the patio. On the other side of the barricade was the staircase that I would walk up to get to my apartment if I wasn't taking the elevator. It was not an easy task to leave the staircase and shimmy around this solid wall and traverse the chest height barrier to my patio.

"They will get over this way," he said with such authority that I believed he had some special knowledge of how this worked.

I was still a little taken aback. I knew the Japanese had a proclivity for buying worn underpants from vending machines but scaling a wall four floors up to claim a random person's clean underwear seemed like a lot of trouble to go to.

"But they will be clean," I said, hearing how comical I sounded to my own ears. Not much embarrassed me, but the ridiculousness of this conversation was surreal.

He chuckled.

"Japanese men aren't picky. They will even take freshly washed panties and either keep them or sell them onward."

It seemed like an inordinate amount of peril to risk for a stranger's newly laundered under garments, but I took one last look over the edge of my patio, deciding at that moment that I would play it safe and hang my panties to dry in my room.

Apart from the low-key threat of underwear thieves, Togoshi Ginza was a bustling but casual shopping street housing a multitude of mom-and-pop shops, ¥100 stores (like dollar stores in the United States), laundromats, tiny eateries, groceries, and more. At the time, it had the dubious distinction of being the longest shopping street in Tokyo. Longest it may have been, but it was by no means the most glamorous. There were no massive window displays sparkling with expensive goods, and the shoppers that dragged their little wheeled shopping carts behind them as they proceeded down the street were simply dressed. If you were standing in the center, though, the parade of tiny shops seemed to stretch on forever in both directions. I really enjoyed living there and spent many lazy afternoons wandering past the open-walled stalls with their cheap patio furniture, home organization bins, school supplies, or other knickknacks on display for perusal by the neighborhood shoppers.

I had been living peacefully in Togoshi for a couple of months at least when someone on the train informed me that they were surprised to hear I was living in Togoshi because it was an "unsafe" neighborhood.

"Where do you all live?" the person had asked us. A stranger on the train platform was making conversation with a group of us.[1]

"Togoshi," I said, not thinking much of it. My friend Carrie, who was with me at the time, also lived in the same building.

"Oh, wow," the guy said. "That's a dangerous neighborhood."

"What?" I replied, thinking about my sleepy neighborhood filled with little old ladies tugging shopping bags on wheels. "No way. It's totally safe."

He gave me a pitying look, as if I had somehow been duped into moving downstairs from a *yakuza* (Japanese gangster) den.

"There was a knifing there," he said.

---

[1] See my essay "I Was a Day-Old Christmas Cake" for an explanation about why this conversation was so unusual.

"A knifing?" It was my turn to give him a speculative look. "I haven't heard of anything like that."

"Look it up," he said, raising an eyebrow.

Prior to this encounter, I already knew that the Japanese litmus test for dangerous, criminal activity was more sensitive than the American equivalent. After all, one of the much-talked about crime sprees spreading across Tokyo as I arrived there was the hot coffee tosser. I'm not sure what the Japanese media actually referred to him as, but the upshot was that we were all warned to be careful of any man stopping his car near us when we were alone. Apparently, a young man in his twenties was driving around Tokyo, pulling up next to young women who were walking by themselves, and throwing hot coffee on them. The impetus for these crimes was apparently that he had been scorned in love and was getting revenge on the female population of Tokyo.[2]

---

[2] The case of the heartbroken coffee tosser was talked about a lot, but I would be remiss if I didn't point out that serious crimes do in fact happen in Japan. In 2007, for instance, a psychologically disturbed teenage boy in Fukushima cut off his mother's head with a saw and carried it around in his backpack for two hours, including during a visit to an Internet cafe, before he turned himself into the police for her murder. Another case that year which made international news was the rape and murder of Lindsay Ann Hawker, a 22-year-old British teacher based in Chiba, by Tatsuya Ichihashi, 28, who was her English student. This case was particularly unusual, since Ichihashi went on the run and managed to evade authorities for over two years before he was finally arrested in 2009. He received life in prison and eventually wrote a book about his life on the run. He never apologized for killing Hawker, but he did say his book was his act of contrition, although I'm not sure how that would be the case, since the book itself only focused on his obsession with hiding and his acts of self-mutilation while running from the police. I have not read it, choosing not to financially support a murderer, but it apparently does not reference Hawker or the murder at all. Finally, Netflix, in 2023,

Given 2008 technology, internet research about a knifing would have to wait until I was home. Back at my apartment, I pulled up Google and entered "Togoshi knifing" into the search query. To my surprise, an article popped up describing the incident.

Now, here is where my memory and an article that I found while searching present day for this incident diverge. I clearly

---

released a documentary titled <u>Missing: The Lucie Blackman Case</u>, about the disappearance of a young British woman working as a hostess in Roppongi, who's disappearance managed to lead the Tokyo Metropolitan Police to uncover the operation of a serial rapist, who's actions had resulted in two deaths, including Blackman's. Joji Obara, a Korean immigrant naturalized as a Japanese citizen and heir to a pachinko-cum-real estate fortune, became involved in organized crime as a money-laundering front for the *Sumiyoshi-kai yakuza* syndicate after his real estate fortune reversed itself. He drugged and raped over 400 young women in Roppongi when he was finally arrested in 2001. Until Blackman's disappearance in 2000, the local Roppongi unit of the Tokyo Metropolitan Police had not taken seriously the reports made by hostesses that they had been drugged and abducted. See my essay "Yakuza-a-Go-Go" for more information on Roppongi and *yakuza* operations there. He ultimately received a life sentence in 2007 for the death of Carita Ridgeway, who died of organ failure related to chloroform toxicity, and then finally, in 2008, for the murder of Lucie Blackman, after a successful appeal by the Blackman family. As a side note to my side note, the Tokyo Metropolitan Police officers that ultimately found Lucie's body created a Shinto shrine at the site where her body was discarded and have visited it every year for the last twenty years to tidy the shrine and pray to her spirit to rest easy. At the end of the day, nothing about my story is intended to diminish these or any other heinous crimes committed by people in Japan. The fact is, however, the average person on the street in Tokyo was more concerned about being hit with hot coffee or being nicked with a pocketknife by a stranger than being murdered by an acquaintance. All that said, however, *gaijin* and Japanese women alike who work the Roppongi hostess scene are likely taking more precautions than the average Tokyo resident.

remember reading about how a distraught kid who had been dumped by his girlfriend had brandished a pen knife at a ¥100 shop that was part of the Togoshi Ginza shopping street. The article made it seem like in his random flailing, he managed to nick a fellow shopper. I remember being amused that this is what constitutes a knifing in Tokyo and instantly dismissed this incident, it clearly not being enough to deem an entire area of Tokyo as "unsafe." I came from a country where even though school shootings were not yet a daily occurrence, as they sadly are now, we had already lived through Columbine, and gun violence was already common enough that a distraught kid swinging a knife in a residential shopping street would not have made national news.

Notwithstanding my memory, the article I pulled up just today from *The Japan Times* indicates that the boy had been "visiting a psychiatric hospital for a few years" and that his attack used two kitchen knives which he brandished while yelling "I will kill you" and "I am not wrong." Relationship troubles were still cited as the source of his motive, but it was not clear that the object of his rage was even present at the store. This article states that two middle-aged females were slightly injured and that three others just had cuts to their clothing.[3]

While this incident is clearly more serious than I remember, it sadly still does not live up to the American expectation for what makes an area dangerous. Heck, there was a gun-related incident outside my neighborhood Publix a few months ago, and I still go

---

[3] Here is a link to the *Japan Times* article, dated January 7, 2008, which I quote in this story:
https://www.japantimes.co.jp/news/2008/01/07/national/teen-assailant-cites-relationship-woes/.

there every week for groceries. I had actually forgotten that any such thing had even occurred until I thought of it just now as I typed this sentence. Despite our abhorrent normalization of rampant gun violence, foreign tourists are being warned by their governments that travel to the United States is dangerous. Yet, we continue to live our lives as if we don't somehow exist in a dystopian hellhole when compared to the relative safety of foreigners in their own home nations.

For instance, per a CNN Travel article posted January 25, 2023, Japanese officials tell their citizens that gun crime is one of the main security concerns in visiting the United States. The Japanese government goes on to offer a lot of advice to its citizens "for getting out of or hunkering down in possible active shooter situations." Advice includes keeping quiet, hiding and barricading doors, and locating security exits. A final bit of advice includes that the Japanese tourist may want to "throw things close to the criminals, use them as weapons."[4]

Having lived in Japan, I absolutely could not imagine the average Japanese citizen confronting an armed assailant, let alone attempting to throw a camera bag, umbrella, or other article at or near a gunman. So as hilarious as I find this advice, it is equally sobering to consider that this is how a country practically devoid of gun violence advises its citizens to act when confronted by a potential situation with an active shooter. To be clear, there will not be time to confront someone who, using a bump stock, can discharge 90 lethal rounds in ten seconds. Your only chance is to flatten yourself against the ground as quickly as humanly possible

---

[4] Here is the link to the CNN Travel article, dated January 25, 2023, which I quote in this story: https://www.cnn.com/travel/article/travel-warnings-other-countries-us-violence/index.html.

and act like you've already been shot. Play dead. You will probably still be shot, but you may get lucky.

The existential horror of this survival advice is not lost on me. I know that if I'm ever in an active shooter situation, it will somehow be simultaneously shocking and completely not unexpected. I take no joy in that knowledge, but I consider myself extremely lucky to have spent five months living in a country where I could walk alone at two in the morning through the center of a city teeming with over thirty-six million individuals and have absolutely no fear of being mugged, raped, or murdered — as long as I stayed clear of Roppongi, that is.[5] The only time I ever feared for my physical safety in Japan was walking past those bars and nightclubs in Roppongi.[6] A girl practically needed to know Aikido to avoid getting grabbed and escorted into some of the establishments by the large African men who served as "bouncers." So, despite the reputation that Togoshi may have had, I always felt completely safe there. I just wish all the neighborhoods in the United States were as dangerous as Togoshi was.

---

[5] As of 2008, the population was approximately 36.3 million people in the greater Tokyo area. As of 2023, this number is now 37.1 million. Via *World Population Review,* https://worldpopulationreview.com/world-cities/tokyo-population.

[6] See my story "Roppongi Redux" for more information about the times I had to visit Roppongi.

AINOTE

I made this ink and watercolor sketch from a photograph I took of the entry gate of Ueno Toshogu and Gojo Tenjin Shrine in Ueno, Tokyo during hanami (cherry blossom viewing) in April 2008 when my sister and I visited Ueno for Hanami

> Scented flowers drift
> soft petals wafting to earth—
> missing *hanami*.

> The bough shakes then quakes,
> bending under the pressure;
> not breaking just yet.

Purple paradox
bathing in an orange sea;
pink shoes kicking north.

A rose blooms at dusk—
ageless in her beauty great
kissed by dappled light.

For that which softly
falls upon the earth, a tear—
even then renews.

Drifting slowly down
through the petals, I see you—
your heart is my home.

A boil of colors
explodes across the expanse—
another sunset.

SALSA ON HOME

Barely having spent a month in Japan, I was already used to being the one stared at on the train, but this particular night in January, I was just a bystander to the drama, not its focus. I couldn't tell if the general mood was concern, annoyance, or amusement among the other passengers. The subtlety of Japanese expression was still largely lost on me at that point in time.

It was the last train of the night, and the few of us aboard were mostly silent, contemplating our evenings or lost in random thought. Carrie and I were on our way home to our guesthouse in Togoshi from visiting friends who lived south of Shinagawa. We had managed to catch the last train to Gotanda on the Tokyu Ikegami Line, one of the smaller lines that connects into Tokyo. In Japan at midnight, when the trains stopped, taxi rates tripled. Often, as a student, if we didn't make it home on the train, we just stayed out until five am when they started running again. In a time before Uber and Lyft, this phenomenon spawned entire enterprises in Tokyo, such as clubs and theme parks open overnight until after the trains restarted in the morning.[1]

---

[1] See "A Labia-Scalding Night on the Town" to learn about a now-defunct but much-loved overnight *onsen* theme park that brought a massive natural spring experience to Tokyo.

Carrie and I chatted in low voices. As *gaijin*, we did not yet understand how exceptionally rude it was to have loud conversations on the train, but it had been a long day, and that evening we were content with quiet conversation or silence. On the bench across from us was a young man sprawled out asleep. It was 2008. He was dressed in a bulky, brightly colored cardigan that could have placed highly in an ugly sweater contest today, as well as jeans rolled up above his ankles and a soft hat shaped like a bowler. And he was snoring, loudly.

Everyone was staring, and by everyone, I mean myself, Carrie, and a few older Japanese people also making their relatively silent journeys home. Every time he shifted, Carrie and I quietly altered our bets on whether he would sleep through his stop. It seems to me that Japanese people have a preternatural ability to detect their station, often appearing to spring directly from a deep meditation and alight from a car without even checking the station name. However, this man was incredibly drunk. He was out cold, taking up half a bench, snoring and drooling. Those were all sins on the train, but cardinal among them was that he didn't have his mobile on silent. It was early 2008, and smart phones were highly uncommon, but most Japanese people had elaborate flip phones that handled email, did video chats, and were equipped with fancy cameras.

Having worked as a software engineer for a telecom company before entering law school, I had heard all about these fabulous high tech Japanese camera phones, and I was not about to miss out on this particular trend. After getting my Japanese identification card, my first act was to run out and buy a wicked mobile phone with a Sony Exilim camera built in, which I used to snap a picture of the public sleeper for posterity. Taking photos of strangers in public was a surprisingly common practice in Japan, despite the extremely reserved nature of Japanese people.

We weren't sure he was truly unconscious, rather than sleeping, until his mobile started ringing. Slumped over on his side, the phone had slipped from his hand to land on the floor of the train car. Every few minutes, it would blare to life, loudly, spewing forth salsa music at a volume deafening in the silent car. The small phone flashed brilliant LEDs and bounced along the floor of the car, vibrating and dancing, as if it alone was still up for a party. The rest of us sure weren't. Then the phone would halt, as if not sure where to move next and remain dark and silent until moved to dance again. The other occupants of the car all looked to each other, trying to decide how to handle the situation.

How is no one checking on this kid? I thought to myself. *Someone's clearly worried about him. The phone keeps ringing, loudly, and no one is waking him up.*

Finally, after a couple of rounds of salsa for your life, an older gentleman assumed the mantle of diplomatic liaison for the group. Keenly aware that this was incredibly awkward, he reluctantly approached the young man.

Oh good, I thought. *He's going to see if he's alright.*

I sighed out a breath in relief, when the older man reached out and patted the sleeping man gently, gingerly, as if the unconscious man might send an electric shock through his bulky and colorful sweater and zap our newly pronounced leader, ending his mission before it even began. The kid shifted and may have mumbled, but his eyes didn't even crack open.

The older gentleman's face remained stoic and unreadable. Meanwhile, the phone began to dance again, as if attempting to entice our leader to pick it up and end the cacophony. Our representative seized this opportunity to more firmly shake the younger man and point to the phone, attempting to focus the kid's attention on the very loud, very saucy mobile. The kid shifted under the man's grasp but still did not awaken. We all sat there, not sure what to do next. It was clear that this kid was not regaining consciousness.

In the United States, maybe we would have just walked off. Maybe we would have left the phone on the ground. Maybe someone would have picked up the phone and picked his pockets, making off with his possessions. Let that be a lesson to him. But I was in Japan, headed home to Togoshi, and that was not how things were in Japan.

Certainly, he's not just going to leave him, I thought. *At least answer the phone the next time it rings and let them know where he is.*

But no, resigned that we were not going to have a quiet ride to our respective stations, the older gentleman picked the phone off the ground, holding it as if it might explode in his hand. It had bounced its way past the young man's feet and partway down the train car floor by then, and the worry wasn't just that it was loud and potentially seizure-inducing in its flashy glory, but that it would get away from the unconscious kid entirely. The older gentleman stuffed the phone into the kid's sweater pocket and sat back down in his seat a bench over.

And so, we waited until the Togoshi-Ginza stop, quiet except for the muffled but exuberant salsa music intermittently blaring unanswered from the sweater pocket of a passed out drunk kid whose drool was forming a puddle on the otherwise spotlessly clean train car bench. Someone was clearly worried about that kid, but no one ever answered the phone, tried again to wake him, or even make noise about whether he was in danger of alcohol toxicity.

Carrie and I got off the train at Togoshi, and the man was still loudly snoring when we did. He was only a couple of stations from the end of the line in Gotanda, and I always wondered if he magically woke up at his stop, or if he'd already snored his way past it, destined to be woken by cleaning staff at Gotanda Station and forced to find a place to sleep for the night or to pay the price for a very expensive taxi ride home. Or maybe they would just let him sleep on the train unmolested until he broke free of his drunken stupor.

I will never know, but it wasn't the habit of the Japanese to interfere in the lives of others or to touch what wasn't theirs. I saw more than one package forgotten in the overhead rack of a car ride untouched from station to station, making its way unshepherded through Tokyo. I also saw more than one man completely passed out, usually salary men, with their Luis Vuitton briefcases used as pillows either on the floor of the train, treating it like a pallet, or crumpled on a Tokyo sidewalk. Let sleeping salary men lie was apparently the rule. Vomit optional.

Once, when a group of my classmates took a selfie with a completely unconscious salary man lying in a pool of his own retch on the sidewalk, I felt sick with shame. At the time, I had thought it was one thing to be culturally appropriate and leave him be, but it was another to treat him as a sideshow. If I'd spoken better Japanese, maybe I would have called the police and gotten them to come help him, but there was never any real threat of danger, and I would come to understand the Japanese better after more time there. No one would steal that Louis Vuitton briefcase. No one would molest him. He could just sleep it off on the street, and Tokyo would pretend it didn't even see him (unless, of course, he had a phone that danced and played loud salsa music every three minutes).

I told myself I wasn't mocking the kid on the train when I took his photo for my travelogue as a way to justify my own social faux pas. Or maybe not a faux pas at all. Sleeping in public doesn't give you any expectation of privacy. I felt slightly bad about it when I posted it on Flickr, but not long after, a Japanese person asked me to add it to the "sleep in public" group, so it appeared I was right on point culturally with how Japanese view private acts in public.

A few months later, in April, when a classmate of mine frantically made out with a Japanese girl in a club in Shibuya, both parties kissing and groping excitedly, twenty pairs of Japanese hands pulled out their mobiles to record a video of the public display of affection. I remember feeling slightly horrified that this girl, who was enjoying a very thorough good time with a handsome *gaijin* might be shamed for it, but I had come to realize that recording the shame of others was a national pastime. The lines are so fine, so delicate. In 2008 America, we might have stolen your wallet, but a massive crowd of strangers probably wouldn't record your random bouts of questionable judgment in a club. Nowadays, Americans are happy to record anything they see in public (or even private) that they might use to shame others.

In 2008, perhaps my horror was just a function of time. I do know this, though. For a culture so intent on fitting into society, shame was the punishment, but it was also the deterrent. Japanese are taught as children that stealing a bicycle might mean never getting a decent job their whole life, so stealing a phone or a package or a briefcase would never even cross the mind of most Japanese people. The fear of shame is omnipresent in Japan, even if it's not dancing on the floor of a train car, whistling its tune for all to hear.

My own public *bushuru* (verb to vomit in an embarrassing public way, literally translated as "to do the Bush thing") happened after acclimating to the Shibuya club scene and the penchant for incredibly weak drinks served at such establishments.[2] Carrie's roommate Matt was charming and sad in the soulful, lost little boy way, and I have always been a complete sucker for such affectations. I had no designs on Matt in that way, but my soft spot for the damaged and pretty was my undoing. That night, Matt was depressed, and he wanted someone to do shots with him. That person turned out to be me, a thirty-year-old who had never been more than buzzed in her life.

I abstained from the usual alcoholic excesses that mark most American kids' undergraduate years, owing primarily to a family propensity for, ironically, shameful acts of public intoxication. The stories and first-hand accounts were more than enough of a deterrent for me in my formative years. That said, I chose a poor time to experiment with shots. After two shots of vodka, Matt took his mild depression and soulful blue eyes back to Togoshi and left the rest of us to dance and enjoy the remainder of the evening. I followed my two shots with a series of incredibly diluted, fruity drinks. It was my usual fare, but the damage was already done. My friend Jennifer had just handed me my third sugary concoction

---

[2] The verb *bushuru* was invented by the Japanese to describe an embarrassing act of public vomiting and came into being in the wake of a very public incident where George H.W. Bush, then president of the United States, vomited in the lap of Japanese Prime Minister Kiichi Miyazawa and then promptly fainted. The incident occurred at Miyzawa's residence, but it was a state dinner and attended by 135 diplomats. Apparently, the President, who came to on the floor under the table with his personal physician, who I guess accompanied him to Japan and told the doctor "Roll me under the table until the dinner's over." This incident of course made international news and ended up on every comedian's lips and eventually parodied on SNL. The President was a good sport about it, but the act itself lives on in the Japanese language.

when I began to feel dizzy. I sat down at one of the chairs at a bar table set up near the dance floor. Dizziness quickly transformed into nausea, and before I could think too hard about it, I was running toward the ladies' room. It was packed with women, and in desperation to get to a toilet, Carrie, who had followed close on my heels, steered me into the men's room.

Despite my distress, the looks of the multiple terrified Japanese men that scrambled wide-eyed from the restroom will be etched in my mind forever. It was as if *Gojira* (Godzilla) himself busted through the door, instead of two female Americans. Carrie pushed me toward the single stall, and I dry-heaved repeatedly into the bowl. Nothing came up, owing to my uncooperative esophagus, but I miserably heaved into the bowl until my guts were tired from straining.

When the heaving subsided, Carrie dragged me out to the landing near the restrooms while she went to collect our coats from the lockers. I slumped against the wall, trying to keep the world from doing its own salsa on the back of my eyeballs when a slim, young Japanese guy with a floppy, shag haircut sidled up next to me. He was wearing tight jeans and the elf-like pointy boot-shoes that the Japanese dude-bros favored at the time.

"*O namae wa desu ka,*" (What is your name?) he asked as he flipped open his phone, ready to type my number.

"*Iie*", (No) I replied shaking my head and waving him away with my arm.[3] I was drunk not stupid. I'm not sure if he was one of the ones who witnessed my gastrointestinal episode in the bathroom, but he clearly thought I was an easy target. I don't know

---

[3] I hadn't yet learned about the finger X, so I made the gauche decision to actually say the word "no." See my essay "Mind the Gap" for an explanation.

what he'd planned to do with my phone number, as my spoken Japanese was leaps and bounds better than my reading or typing, and Japanese people communicated primarily via mobile email, but I didn't even bother to ask.[4] He slunk away with his phone as Carrie approached me with our coats.

    She pulled me down the stairs and out the front door of the club, guiding me toward the train station. In a stroke of dubious luck, I had magically timed my drunken sickness with the five am timeline for the trains restarting, and we only had to wait twenty minutes for the first train of the day. I retched again in the plants on a street corner and again in a trash bin inside the station, to no avail. I would have to sleep this one off. Unlike the young Japanese man sleeping on the train a couple months back, none of my friends took a photo of me, and I made it home safe, no missed station, and no salsa music to disrupt the locals. Whether anyone captured me on their phone retching into the men's room toilet, I'll never know.

---

[4] Back then, the per minute cost to call someone on a mobile phone was astronomically high in Japan, so you only spoke it if was necessary. Pretty much everyone just emailed each other on their phones.

AINOTE

I made this ink and <u>watercolor</u> sketch from a photograph I took in January, 2008 of the Kamakura Daibatsu (Giant Buddha) dated 1252 located in Kamakura, the ancient capital of Japan

> My words flow freely—
> time and space and sadness pass,
> like sand through fingers.

Inside the fertile
garden of my mind, I walk
and dream of days gone.

Anxiety and
relief—simultaneous,
inexplicably.

Smashing through my heart
and now running through my head,
is yesterday's pain.

Rabbit hole—
my mind wanders aimless, yet
ever vigilant.

Robot wings collide,
but metal fangs click away—
grip the sky today.

Winged sentiments—

swirling gently in the breeze;
lost beneath the moon.
Raucous rain splashes
down on the world around,
leaving droplets here.

NO TIME FOR LOVE, DOCTOR JONES!

If I could go back in time, perhaps the one thing I would have changed about my time in Tokyo is that I would have broken up with my partner before I left the United States. It doesn't make me proud to say this, especially since this relationship lasted another seven years after I left Japan, but I think it would have entirely changed my outlook during the trip and provided an opportunity to spend some time alone with the latitude to internalize even more fully who I was as a person without the artificial context of someone else in the background.

We had only been dating about five months when I moved to Japan, and this relationship essentially occurred right after I left another relationship that had lasted ten years. I jumped right into it with my partner having not really experienced being alone with my own mind since I was the age of nineteen. Now at thirty, I had never really gotten to explore myself as an adult without having to fit that image of myself into a picture with another person there. That wasn't my partner's fault, but it definitely contributed to our issues.

Ironically, this was already a lot of baggage to have collected in 2008, but since then, my relationship issues have not to my dismay gotten less complicated. All the intervening years aside, I've attempted to start this essay at least three separate ways, each time digging a little bit deeper and making myself a little more uncomfortable. The hard facts of it are that my partner at the time was not supportive of my experiences in Japan. It manifested as controlling behavior, derision if I made a mistake, and often culminated in a judgmental statement that perhaps I wasn't mature enough to be with them. All these reactions stemmed from jealousy. At the time I thought it was about my interactions with other people, but looking back, and knowing what I know now, after fifteen years, deep down I know it was because my partner was jealous that they didn't get to be me and have the experience that I had living in Tokyo.[1] Every social picture I took that might have a

---

[1] This seems like the appropriate time to mention that my partner, in 2008, was a closeted trans woman, something that she would not admit to herself at the time, and that I would not learn for another four years. After she transitioned, we were together for another three years before she left me. I fully appreciate that she was grappling with a lot of complex feelings both about herself and what she wanted from life and me, as someone that she later used as a basis for determining her path into womanhood. Even when we first started dating and she was presenting as a cis heterosexual male, she had a lot of complex expressions and feelings about me and my role as the perfect avatar for what she wanted to be. So, when she came down on me for not behaving like she would have in any given situation, I think it was more her frustration for not being able to "take the wheel" as it were in her own life rather than a misogynistic need to be controlling of mine. I neither excuse nor accept her behavior when it was toxic, but I understand it. Every person has their own battle to fight, and hers was particularly tough. Throughout this book, I need to honor my own experiences and the feelings they provoked, both then and now, but I do this as respectfully as possible, because we all deserve to be respected on a fundamental level, even when we are less than gracious in our behavior.

guy in it resulted in a fight. Even my drunken sickness at the Shibuya club was painted as being incredibly immature and reckless, and my partner called into question whether they should be with someone who made such bad decisions. I was the problem. Instead of sympathy or even amusement, I was berated. It was a lot of pressure to feel from someone 7,500 miles away.

During my semester in Tokyo, my partner traveled to Japan to visit me twice. The first time was in February, in time for Valentine's Day, with the itinerary focused in and around Tokyo, and the second time was after my semester ended. In May, we started in Tokyo and then traveled around Kyoto and Hakone during Golden Week.[2] The February visit occurred while still in the

---

On to housekeeping: when the events of this book took place, my partner was not presenting as female. I will never dead name her or use male pronouns that are completely inaccurate to her sense of self, but I also want to be true to my own experience from this time, so I will refer to her as my "partner" and use the pronouns "they" in retelling stories that involve her. As a final note of housekeeping, I also had one friend during this time who was already transitioned, and she will just be "she/her" throughout this book. Since 2008, I have had another friend from this time come out as transgender and begin the process of transitioning. As her gender at the time the stories involving her took place was not something that changed my experience, I will only refer to her as her chosen name and preferred pronouns throughout.

[2] Golden Week, *Ogon Shukan* in Japanese, is one week every year between April 29 and May 5. A large majority of Japanese people have off during this week because this one single week encompasses four separate national holidays in Japan. As usual, the Japanese are efficient, even in giving themselves time off! It's a time of massive travel and holiday congestion, because for many Japanese people, it is the longest stretch of time they might have off in any given year. Ironically, the name Golden Week came from a Japanese film company that dubbed it Golden Week because movie ticket sales spiked during that time and similar listener spikes in radio broadcasts were referred to as "golden time". See, capitalist America isn't the only one to

thick of one of these major fights. I think they were still upset about the club incident, but it could have been anger about a photo of me sitting next to a fellow student, Houston, that made its way onto Facebook. Carrie, Becky, and I visited Houston, Patrick, and Allen to grab a quick dinner in their neighborhood in south of Shinagawa, and someone snapped a photo where Houston had an arm around my shoulder, which was the source of my partner's anger. The pose was entirely a function of the photographer taking a snap of us at dinner. Houston and I weren't even sitting close enough to be touching except for the moment I leaned over for the photo, and he slung his arm behind me and to my shoulder. The photo making its way to Facebook, however, incited atomic rage.

Whatever the reason was, my partner arrived ahead of Valentine's Day angry at me. Crossed arms, frowns, one-word responses, and biting sarcasm were the whole menu for the first few days. That didn't mean we didn't have a lot of sex. It just meant I had to put up with a shitty attitude and someone who didn't appreciate the cookies I tried to bake in the toaster oven of my minuscule kitchen. For context, Japanese tradition dictates that on Valentine's Day, every woman should buy the men in her life chocolate. The men do not reciprocate the chocolate until White Day.[3]

---

name events after profits! If you are traveling to Japan for holiday, I recommend going early April so that you can enjoy the confluence of cherry blossoms, good weather, and no Golden Week! That said, if you are traveling with the specific goal of climbing Mt. Fuji, go after July 1, but before September 10, otherwise you will be disappointed. I wasn't there when Fuji-san was open, so that is one adventure I will have to go back for.

[3] There is a dedicated phrase for all of this candy that women are expected to buy for every man in their lives, even their bosses and coworkers. It's called *giri choco*, which translates into "obligation chocolate". I find it

For her lover, a Japanese woman might bake something or buy something high quality, which is referred to as *honmei choco* or "true feeling chocolate". My attempt at *honmei choco* was pretty squarely rebuffed, and it wasn't until a few days into the two-week visit that the groveling (peace-making, really, since I know I didn't have anything for which to apologize) and angry sex transitioned into make-up sex and finally broke the tension enough for us to get on with the actual trip. Among some of the awesome stuff on our itinerary, including a visit to the Ghibli Museum, a nice dinner at ShabuZen, trips to Japanese art museums, and hilarious *purikura* (literally translated as photobooth, but often used to describe the

---

hilarious that this obligation chocolate is purchased en masse each year by women to show appreciation for all the men in their lives but is in fact quite literally named obligation chocolate. To give you an understanding of how widespread this practice was in 2008, please note that approximately 70% of the annual revenue of Japanese confectionaries has historically come from Valentine's sales of obligation chocolate. In the year 2005, approximately $600 million in 2022 dollars was spent on obligation chocolate. The year before I visited, in 2007, the average woman spent $50 in 2022 dollars on obligation chocolate, although by 2019, that number has dropped to an average of about $10 per woman. Finally waking up that this practice might be putting undue pressure on women to show affection for male coworkers and superiors that such women might not feel, some companies have gone so far as to ban the practice of giving and receiving *giri choco*, replacing it with optional *tomo choco*, or "friendship chocolate" given just to friends. Per a 3M survey, the percentage of women who purchase obligation chocolate seems to have dropped from an average of 80% of women surveyed in 2007 to only 40% as of 2017. When I was there in 2008, obligation chocolate was everywhere, and it was way more ubiquitous than the chocolates advertised for White Day, which is the reverse day where men buy women chocolate, and falls on March 14. Feel free to check out the Wikipedia page on *giri choco* to dig deeper into this bizarrely sexist custom. (Https://en.wikipedia.org/wiki/Giri_choco)

stickers that are dispensed by the booth), we knew we wanted to visit a love hotel. However, we didn't actually make it to a love hotel until my partner's second trip to Tokyo, in May.

During my time living in Tokyo, I don't think I spent any days there where I wasn't touched by at least ten or more strangers as I made my way around, usually on the train, or squeezing through crowded streets. It got so frequent that by the time I left, I craved space more than anything else. Personal space, anonymity, and the ability to not fear being groped in public (called *chikan* in Japanese) places were at the top of the list. I was also eager to be away from my born-again Australian roommate who seemed to both dislike me and try to chat me up if he thought I was awake behind the *shoji* that separated my room from the tiny kitchen, the door sliding open almost at the sink. It didn't matter to him if the screen was closed or not. Even sharing a guesthouse with strangers meant never really being alone.[4]

When my partner visited at the end of the semester, things were much less tense, and we decided to have a laugh by checking

---

[4] My relationship with my roommate was a complex one, but ultimately it was minor to my experience living in Japan. Less than 2% of the Japanese population is Christian, with the vast majority identifying as either Shinto, Buddhist, or both. As of 2008, my roommate had been stuck in Japan for 12 years, having purchased a one-way ticket from Australia for temporary work and then been unable to afford to go home. He worked a series of menial jobs, lived in guesthouses, and lost over a decade to a subsistence life in Japan. He found God only a couple of years before I met him, and I truly think it was a coping mechanism for him to combat the isolation of being a *gaijin* in a country he both loved but didn't want to be trapped in. It was a way to find other foreigners to interact with, but the result was that he was very judgmental about Americans, and he applied those generalizations to me on a whim with no understanding of how vastly diverse America is.

out the love hotel I had been eyeing online. By then, I had come to understand the bone-deep anxiety of feeling like I was never actually alone, that need to breathe completely unobserved that encapsulates at least partly the reason such hotels exist in Japan.

The idea sprang up because the need for privacy doesn't just apply to me living in Japan. It applies to everyone in the entire country. Most families live three generations in a single house, often sharing bedrooms. A married couple may sleep in the same room as their children or their parents. Thus, the love hotel industry saw the need for alone time and filled the gap with numerous hotels that cater to couples seeking a private place to fuck. These hotels are available in two-hour blocks and are designed to provide a place where individuals and couples can go for privacy. I once remember reading that upwards of 30% of people who visit love hotels aren't even there for sex. Some just want somewhere quiet to read or watch TV or just be alone without anyone around them for a couple of hours.

My partner and I found the novelty of the pay-by-the-hour hotel and the idea that you pick your room from a vending machine and never see another person while you're there to be too interesting not to make it onto the Tokyo activity wish-list. One of the kitschy things about love hotels is that each room is usually decorated around its own theme and is unique inside that hotel. No cookie cutter rooms here! After looking up a few online, we made the trek into Shibuya which was home to a large selection of these establishments. We chose to visit the P&A Plaza Art Hotel in Shibuya. Sadly, my first choice of room was already taken, the button dimmed as we perused the options. I remember it had an elaborate rock shower and bath. We ended up snagging a Moroccan style room with inlaid tables, diaphanous pillow covers, and a tiled bathroom. The vending machine displayed a photo of each room on a large panel of buttons. I'm sure it's since been updated to giant touch panels, but in 2008, it was large plastic buttons with a photo. If the room was lit up, it was available for rent. The occupied rooms would be darkened. Once you fed your yen into the machine and selected a room, the key would dispense through the bottom of the machine. From there, you traversed entirely empty elevators and hallways to find your room.[5]

The room we selected felt palatial in size compared to the average Tokyo room. Most of the bells and whistles were operated via a computer panel inside, including the window shades, television, lights, vibration of the bed, etc. The walls were painted in earthy tones of orange and yellow with small wrought iron sconces and a velvet neck roll along the back of the bed. The bathroom had a large white enamel circular tub on a tiled platform nestled against a terra cotta colored wall, and the toiletries included for our use were ridiculously expansive, such as hair gel, lotion, bubble bath, and more. It was well beyond the meager selection of necessities offered by a standard hotel. Inside the room was another vending machine with the label "Fashion Shopping" that dispensed sex toys, lubes, and anything else we might have needed that was too expensive or personal to be offered for free. It also had snacks! From one vending machine, we could get a rabbit vibrator for ¥5000 ($50) or a cup-o-noodles for ¥200 ($2). The room itself was like a mini theme park for sexual activity. At the same time, it was

---

[5] Not many establishments took credit cards in Japan in 2008, although I could pay my rent via credit card. It was a very cash-focused society. Contactless didn't exist, of course, but even chip and pin or basic card readers were rare. I'm super curious as to whether that has changed, particularly following COVID, and I suspect that it has. Back in the day, though, you just carried around tons of cash and used it wherever you went.

super quiet and peaceful. You couldn't hear any noise, which if you've ever been to Tokyo, you know that is a feat in and of itself.

For a long time, we just puttered around, pushing all the buttons, exclaiming over the features and marveling at the fact that it felt like a high-tech bordello invented by a horny teenage boy. I think in the end we almost felt obligated to have sex since we were at the love hotel. There was something hilarious and yet intensely uncomfortable in the expectation created by the room itself. This glorious parody of intimacy took a bow and offered everything we could possibly need to make it happen, and it did happen, but underneath the glitz was this energy that if we didn't utilize the room for its intended purpose, we would somehow be insulting the establishment itself.

We made use of the giant circular, jetted bathtub first. It could have held three or more people and was perhaps designed to approximate a private *onsen* (Japanese hot spring), which we filled with bubbles. The entire experience had that slightly clinical feel that all Japanese attempts at hospitality retain. More than just an air of formality was a precision that made you feel like moving a bottle of shower gel half an inch would be a total disruption to the aesthetic that the careful hotel staff had achieved. It was a mentally intense environment. All Japanese hotels have aesthetic precision, from the *ryokan* (traditional Japanese inn) with crisply folded *futon* (mattress frequently folded and set to the side during the day) and perfectly arranged *kotatsu* (low table with a heater underneath) to the modern Western-style hotels with singing toilets, automated blinds, and heated mirrors that don't steam up, but there is something so destabilizing about entering an aesthetically precise environment with the knowledge that the point is to be disruptive and personal and dirty.

If you're reading this and thinking, *Wow, this is not nearly as hot as I thought it would be describing an experience at a love hotel!* That is exactly the point! It just wasn't hot. It wasn't sad or unsatisfying or unsuccessful, but it wasn't hot. It was interesting, amusing, entertaining, and ultimately just a little disquieting.

I know that some people just go to love hotels to have alone time, but to this day, I can't fathom how that environment could possibly have made me feel relaxed enough to ignore the bells and whistles of the high-tech bordello and focus on the quiet and calm of the room. It felt like walking into a well-appointed pressure cooker complete with performance expectations and the conflicting sensations that disruption or a failure to disrupt would result in equal disappointment. Followers of Shinto believe that every object has a *kami* (a spirit or god that oversees it), and that *Yaoyorozu no Kami* (translated as "eight million gods" but conceptually means infinite gods) exist to cover all manner of organisms and physical objects in both the natural and man-made world. Maybe my experience at P&A Plaza just reflected restive *kami*, or maybe it was my own brain telling me that my inner needs weren't being met, so how could such an experience possibly be pressure-free. Looking back, it feels like I should have known all along that my time in Tokyo was never meant for romantic love. It was meant for exploration and growth. Maintaining the status quo was not the right move, but, as they say, it's always easier to look back than to look forward.

AINOTE

I made this ink and watercolor sketch from a photograph I took of Himeji Castle, also called Shirasagi-jo (White Heron Castle) in Himeji, Hyogo Prefecture in March 2008

Blinking hard against
the intense blue of the day—
sinks through me to earth.

A sigh whistles through
the wall of my chest in—out
and to the ether.

Peonies grow in
the place inside my heart that
your love inhabits.

Bird song fills the air,
jasmine scent on the night breeze—
your hand touches mine.

To breathe in and out
is to wait for sleep to come—
eyes fixed to the sky.

THAT TIME THE TRAIN WAS DELAYED

I waffled on whether to keep the title of this story as-is, but train delays are so incredibly rare in Japan, that this is about as momentous as this title gets. Fifteen years after the incident in question, I thought I would do some research to determine if there was more context I could learn after-the-fact, since the experience itself was pretty much third-party hearsay translated by people who spoke little English from a garbled train announcement system with little to no corroboration from anyone at the time. I didn't think to look up the incident the next day in The Japan Times, the primary English paper in Japan in 2008.

Incredibly, in searching around for derailments at the general time I recall the incident occurring, I came across details on the website for the Japan Transport Safety Board (JTSB), which meticulously tracks all occurrences of rail issues and publishes reports for major incidents and archives them online in both Japanese and English. There are three major Japanese rail accidents that seem to come up with a general internet search, two of which are derailments. The first is the Matsukawa derailment in the middle of the night on August 17, 1949, in which a passenger train flipped over and killed three crew members near Fukushima. The second is the Tsunami rail accident on November 9, 1963, outside Yokohama, where two passenger cars collided with a derailed freight train resulting in 162 fatalities. The third is the Amagasaki derailment in Hyōgo Prefecture, in Western Japan, that occurred just after rush hour on April 25, 2005. This particular accident was horrific, in that the first two cars of the train derailed and hit an apartment building. 106 passengers and the driver died and 562 others were injured.

You may read this and think, *Shit, I didn't know trains in Japan are so dangerous*! Well, really, they are absolutely not dangerous. They are incredibly safe, in fact. In its reporting on the year 2008, the JTSB indicates that there were a total of seven derailments across the entire country of Japan, none of which had any casualties, and only one of which rose to the level of requiring a published report. Consider first the number of trains running all across Japan. From the intercity trainlines, to the local lines, to the *shinkansen* (bullet trains), the total number of train cars in operation as of 2022 exceeded 60,000. Japan Railways, only one of the major passenger train operators, runs 26,000 train trips on an average day just on its own. So, you see that the mishaps are infinitesimally small. I don't know why I love all these random train facts, but you'll have to bear with me, because I just wanted to point out how incredibly unlikely it was that I was riding a train at the specific moment that it was impacted by an incident on the lines.

February in Tokyo is pretty solidly into the winter season. If you've never been to Japan, the climate can be approximated to Washington, D.C., which is why the Japanese government chose to gift the United States with a bunch of *sakura* trees, since they would bloom on relatively the same schedule in D.C. as they do in

Japan.[1] It doesn't snow frequently in Tokyo, although the northern island of Hokkaido is known for its snow and excellent skiing.[2] In

---

[1] My grandmother, who grew up on a farm in central D.C. told me this, and I love the notion so much that I can't bring myself to fact-check it. In this one specific instance, believing this might be true means more to me than accuracy. As of this writing, my grandmother just turned 98, and this random potential fact is my way of honoring her. So, don't bother correcting me if I'm wrong. As an aside, my grandmother has a complex relationship with the Japanese people herself. She oscillates between love of the *sakura* trees all around D.C. to hatred born from her revulsion related to the acts of the Japanese military during World War II. She was present at the Navy Commission trial for war crimes of multiple Japanese military personnel, including Lt. General Tachibana, Lt. Col. Ito, Rear Admiral Sakaibara, Surgeon Captain Hiroshi Iwanami, Rear Admiral Shimpei Asano, and Surgeon Commander Chisato Ueno. These individuals committed myriad atrocities, including torture, murder, cannibalism, and even medical experimentation, often done on American or civilian POWs. At the time the trials began, my grandmother was 19 years old and serving as a secretary to one of the Generals on base, so she was asked to take shorthand of the proceedings, including the testimony of witnesses and the statements of the Japanese officials themselves. Did this experience influence her feelings? Absolutely. Fairly? Perhaps not, but deeply still.

[2] I recently learned that Hokkaido's capital, Sapporo, is a sister city for Portland, Oregon. I recently had occasion to visit Portland and visited the Portland Japanese Garden. It was a very interesting experience, as I visited several gardens while living in Japan, many of which were deeply historical around the temples of Kyoto. My sense of being in the Portland Japanese garden is that it is simultaneously nothing like a Japanese garden in many regards but also intimately recognizable as Japanese at the same time. It isn't the elements in the garden that give it the same spirit as a garden in Japan but rather the relationship of those elements to each other. I highly recommend visiting if you get the chance. Also, it was very educational to learn more about Japanese garden design from an English-speaker in English, which I did not have the opportunity to do while living in Japan.

2008, though, we had what people in Tokyo considered to be a snowy year. There were scattered days of snow in the city, and I even recall that I skipped the *Setsubun* festivities due to crappy weather.³ *Setsubun* falls pretty early in the year but is considered a

---

³*Setsubun* is a Shinto festival that marks the Japanese calendar's demarcation for the day before spring starts and typically falls on February 3rd. I wouldn't call that spring, but the Japanese do their own thing regarding the seasons… well, in this case, they do the Chinese thing, because it originated with a Chinese custom, *tsuina*, first introduced to Japan in the 700s. *Tsuina* is the Chinese practice of expelling demons in an exorcism through dance, sacrifices, or other rituals as determined by whichever Taoist sect was performing the exorcism. Modern *Setsubun* traditions, however, date to the *Muromachi* period, which was between 1336 and 1573, and began as a tradition of the aristocracy and *samurai* class of citizens, who would throw beans out their windows to ward off evil spirits. This practice was based on a 10th century legend about a monk binding a demon (or *oni* as they are called in Japanese — no commonality between *oni* and what Christianity calls demons, but there you are) with roasted beans. That original monk was clearly a wise man, understanding even then that that we are all demons before our morning coffee! Apparently, however, soy were the beans of choice to drive off demons because of a cute Japanese word trick whereby the same word for bean, *mame*, can be also written using kanji that translates to demon's eye. So, I guess, the monk's thought was… accost the *oni* with the flaming eyeballs of its brethren and you will drive it away. Clearly this was metaphorical rather than literal, but the practice caught on, and by the Edo period, everyone in Japan was throwing beans here, there, and everywhere during *Setsubun*. There are some other more smelly traditions that go along with *Setsubun*, but the parades and public observation tends to focus on any number of individuals donning *oni* masks and costumes and running around letting the general public pelt them with beans, in a ritual known as *mamemaki* (which literally translates to bean roll — or bean scattering if we're going by the functional translation). At individual homes, just like in the old legend, roasted soybeans are tossed out the doors and windows and thrown at any unsuspecting person playing the part of the household's *oni* with the exclamation of *Oni wa soto!*

beginning-of-spring festival. By late February, we were still having these snowy days, but my friends Becky and Erin and I were determined to get out, and I asked them if they fancied a trip up to Nikkō. My father, in giving me information about a family visit he took to Tokyo when he was a child, insisted that I should get up to Nikkō, north of Tokyo, because that was where the original carving of The Three Wise Monkeys was housed.

He didn't give me much to go on as far as location, but I managed to look up Nikkō and see that the Tōshō-gū shrine at the Rinnō-ji Temple did indeed appear to be a major draw to the Nikkō area.[4] I don't know if they really are the first pictorial representation of *Mizaru* (see not), *Kikazaru* (hear not), and *Iwazaru* (speak not), but they are definitely the most popular depiction in Japan. the maxim itself is a subset drawn from the broader philosophy of Confucius. Why monkeys, you didn't ask? Well, the Japanese do love their word play. In this case, for example,

---

Fuku wa uchi! (Devils out! Fortune In!) The common practice is to then slam the door in the *oni*'s face for good measure. I'm kind of sad that I missed out on this mass-door-slamming tradition due to weather, but I still think about what it probably looks like, and it brings a smile to my face.

[4] In all fairness, Tōshō-gū has other reasons to visit. It was built in 1617, during the Edo period, and the shrine is dedicated to Tokugawa Ieyasu, the founder of the Tokugawa shogunate, which was the political system governing feudal Japan on which all those *shōgun* books, pop culture movies and angsty and misogynistic but still fantastic Kurosawa films are based. He was a pretty big deal. His bones rest at Tōshō-gū, and the whole compound is an UNESCO World Heritage Site. That said, I honestly was there to see the monkeys, so I'm not going to pretend that I was exploring history and having deep thoughts about Japan's political isolation during the reign of the *shōgun* leading to its eventual collapse and the rise of the Meiji restoration. Feel free to pick up a history book if that's your jam! This is all about the monkeys, baby!

the regular form of the verb "to see" is *miru*. *Mizaru* is the formal form of the negative conjugation of the verb to see. Hence, "see not". But *zaru* is also a modified form of *saru* which means "monkey". The references to see not, hear not, speak not, and monkeys are literal. The evil, however, that's implied.

So, despite the cold and potential for snow if we headed north, Becky, Erin and I decided to put on our bulkiest coats and catch the Tōbu Nikkō Line from the Asakusa station not far from our school toward Nikkō. All our classes were held in the evenings, so we had days free to embark on such mini-adventures, or, you know… get a job. With respect to my situation, you could either say I was lazy and already had a job set up for Summer 2008 so had no need to scramble and get a resume booster, or you could instead posit that I was super industrious and had worked hard my first whole year of law school and then during on-campus interviews in the previous Fall to secure a job for the next Summer and thus was way ahead of the game and entitled to goof off and enjoy Japan.[5]

---

[5] It's worth noting that the 2008 financial crisis began while I was in Tokyo with the failure of Bear Stearns on March 13 and then Lehman Brothers after I left and continually got worse for all of us budding lawyers during my final year of law school. I ended up being deferred from starting my full-time position as a lawyer by nine months. Interestingly, my International Financial Transactions professor in Tokyo worked for Lehman at the time and gave us an excellent primer on structured finance with first-hand examples of how the liquidity crunch drove Bear Stearns under. It was really quite interesting for those of you who are economics nerds like me and probably not at all to anyone else. At the time, he was perhaps too snobby about how wise and great Lehman was, and how it would never go the way of Bear Stearns. I guess my professor was either in denial or didn't know exactly how much of Lehman's portfolio was held in housing-related assets. Yeah… so, it filed for bankruptcy on September 15, 2008, but by then my professor had wisely jumped ship to Ernst & Young. Professorial drama aside,

Either way, I wasn't seeking a job, so I used my time to explore and take in the culture. Also, it was a Sunday!

Unlike the Japan Rail trains, the Tōbu Nikkō Line was not super modern. It was one of the older subway-style cars with rows of orange and yellow patterned fold-down seats lining the long walls of the car and facing inward. Nikkō was the last stop on the line, and it should have taken us about an hour to ride the 100 kilometers (62ish miles for you Imperial-only folks). Our car only had a few other passengers on it, since it was late morning and, as mentioned, a Sunday. We sat together, chatting about nonsense at a volume definitely above the level considered polite by Japanese train etiquette standards. It was still February. We hadn't quite picked up the rule about loud talking on trains. As we traveled north, the environment outside of the train went from tiny bits of icy snow here and there to visible accumulations.

I may have mentioned at some point that I live in Florida. As a person who lives in Florida, I don't see snow unless I'm traveling. I could give you some spiel about how magical the earth looks with a light blanket of beautiful, white snow on it, but let's be real here. My first memories as a child include literal walls of packed snow. I was born in Brooklyn, NY in 1977 to two newly minted doctors. A few months after my birth, my parents moved us to Buffalo so that they could complete their residencies at Buffalo General Hospital. Snow was a huge part of my early life. Donning snowsuits

---

it probably would have been wise to seek employment in Tokyo, even if I already had a job lined up back home, but, even then, the 2008 financial debacle impacted the whole world, so it probably wouldn't have made a difference anyway. Ultimately, I treasure my experience in Japan as the cultural exploration that it was, and if I'd spent all my days working for Sega or Panasonic, I would probably have a very different and arguably less entertaining set of stories to tell about my experience.

to go to daycare. Climbing the cliff of snow in the driveway that led to the front yard. Breaking icicles off the roof and sucking on them like popsicles. Hey, we Gen Xers have awesome immune systems, ok! I even remember taking a hammer and hacking off chunks of ice from the thick layer that comprised the top of the "yard"—an accumulation which was a few feet thick—so that we could throw "snowballs" at each other. It was too cold to even make snowballs, so we had to improvise with ice chunks. In fact, the reason I live in Florida now is because my mother insisted that we move somewhere warm after Buffalo, so you can even blame the fact that I'm sitting here with a heat index of 101 while I wait for Hurricane Idalia to make landfall on the potentiality that I've seen too much fucking snow in my life already. In the end, me having experienced Niagara Falls frozen over as a child meant that a light blanket of snow as we headed north to Nikkō was not all that impressive, but it was still pretty.

We were perhaps two-thirds of the way through our journey to Nikkō when the train came to a screeching halt. I've never been in a train that stopped short like that before. The Tōbu Nikkō line was not a bullet train and was likely only traveling between 45 and 50 mph when we clattered to a noisy halt.[6] Even so, my friends and I had to grab the bars and benches to keep from being jolted from our seats. What followed immediately after was a cacophony of questions echoing around the car in both English and Japanese. The car was at a complete standstill with no station in sight. Our surroundings weren't even urban by that point in the trip, just scraggly trees and low foliage with snow collected on the ground. We were still recovering our bearings when the train's intercom clicked to life and a garbled rush of Japanese crackled through the

---

[6] The trains on the Tōbu line max out at 100 km/h (or 62 mph).

speakers into our car. Erin, Becky, and I looked at each other. I knew the most Japanese out of the three of us, but it was too broken and too fast for me to even attempt to follow. It was also much too long to be a normal train announcement. I felt uneasy as I shook my head, indicating that I didn't know what it was about.

Erin approached one of the other passengers in our car, who was sporting a mildly panicked look and asked, in her calm voice, what the announcer had said. She pointed at the speaker, and the passenger seemed to understand the question. She said something in Japanese, and then asked around among the other passengers, until they collectively found someone able to give us some type of explanation.

"Another train in front—came off the track. Train delay."

"Thank you," Erin replied. "How long?"

The man shook his head. He didn't know.

"A train ahead of us derailed?" I asked.

"That's what they think," she said. "Based on the announcement."

"Oh my god," I said. "It's going to take forever to clear the track. There's no way we're going to get to Nikkō."

We looked around at each other uneasily, concerned not just about arriving at our destination, but about what would happen if we were forced to disembark and find alternate transport. The passengers were similarly agitated, talking amongst themselves rapidly in Japanese, even between groups that weren't traveling together. There is nothing like a crisis to break all sense of rigid social strictures. One man eventually got up and walked to the end of the car and through the door into the next car. It was the first time I had ever seen a Japanese person walk between cars, which they almost never seem to do. I suspected he was going to consult others about what was going on, or maybe the driver directly.

The rest of us waited around, pacing back and forth, or staring out the window trying to see if there was anything we could spot outside the window. Eventually, the man who'd left the car returned, and all the Japanese people began talking again. They spoke for a long time but didn't seem to come to any resolution. They were nice enough to fill us in on the lack of news.

"Waiting," the English speaker said. "Nothing changes."

We nodded back, but the energy in the car was still tense. We were all clearly safe, but we also felt stranded, and Erin, Becky, and I were particularly worried that we might have to call the school to figure out what to do to get back.

Time seemed to drag as the car stayed completely still. The lights and environmental controls kept running, so it wasn't as if we had died on the tracks, but it was static. We all collectively jumped when, about only fifteen minutes into our marooning, the speakers crackled to life again, and another message assaulted us in hurried, warped Japanese. Every single passenger went bolt still and silent, every ear pricked to the message. It must have been good news, because when it ended, the chatter picked up again, and people were smiling and nodding.

"We go now," our translator informed us. "Train will move."

"Really?" Erin asked.

The person nodded in a bow, and Erin thanked him again.

She was clearly as dubious as I was that they were able to clear the tracks so quickly. Did they just have cranes waiting around everywhere? The other passengers seemed very confident, however, so we took our seats and held our breath as we waited those last moments it took for the driver to prepare for our departure. The passenger was correct, however, and, less than a minute later, our car began to screech as it was dragged into forward momentum. We started slowly and picked up speed until we were traveling at the usual speed for travel. The three of us kept an eye on the windows to see if we would pass any wreckage or emergency vehicles or anything that might indicate an accident, but we didn't pass anything of the sort and arrived in Nikkō without further ado, only about twenty minutes later than the projected arrival time.

We had a lovely time in Nikkō, even with the snow and stress of travel, and our return trip was completely uneventful. Looking back, I don't understand why I didn't try to look up what happened after the fact, but I guess we just assumed that the Japanese were somehow superheroes of efficiency in their train management and were fully capable of dealing with a derailment in record time. The reality is that we were nowhere near the accident, but that the authorities took the precaution of freezing all the trains in the area until they could assess the situation and confirm that it didn't pose a risk for any other passenger trains that day. In looking back at the JTSB's reports from 2008, at 9:54 am (not published until June 2009), the outbound local 909S train, which was only three cars, traveling from Ofuna station bound for Shonan Enoshima on the Enoshima line, departed the Shonan Fukasawa station at its normal time of 9:50 am.

All seemed fine until a point at which, upon departing from Shonan Fukasawa, the train was accelerating unnaturally and continued to accelerate even though the driver had not set the train's controller to cause the acceleration. It approached the next station, Nishi Kamakura, with inadequate braking force and even the application of the emergency break and a separate security break by the driver did not stop the train quickly enough. The train blew through the station's designated stop point and collided with the turnout (the railway switch that moves the tracks and diverts trains on different tracks) outside the station. At this point, the stopped train's position was in the way of the approaching inbound local 904S train. Apparently, because the 904S train was thirty seconds behind schedule leaving the Kateseyama station, the driver of the 904S train was able to apply an emergency break and stop the train 19 m short of the damaged and disabled 909S train. Because of a thirty second delay on the schedule of train 904S, the 22 passengers and 2 crew members of the 909S train, and the 16 passengers and 2 crew members of the 904S train all survived with no injuries.

The findings report published by the JTSB speculate that electromagnetic noise interfered with the communications between the master controller used by the driver and the VVVF inverter equipped on the train. A VVVF inverter (also called a propulsion inverter) is the control device that converts the DC power coming in from the train's power source to AC power and regulates the voltage and frequency supplied to the train. The inverter is what's responsible for a smooth launch, acceleration, deceleration and stopping of a train. So, basically, electrical noise interfered with the communication between this inverter and the controller, and the wrong instructions were communicated to the inverter, causing the train to accelerate abnormally and to not brake at the driver's direction. The JTSB, in its report, went on to make some recommendations on how to avoid a similar occurrence in the future, including that drivers should immediately break when they notice an abnormal acceleration, no matter how far they are from the next station, that railway operators should put additional grounding measures in place to reduce the potential for electromagnetic noise, potential upgrades to the watch dog software that monitors the safety of the braking systems in the trains, and finally put into place a process to record these potential abnormalities even if no incident occurs so that they can better investigate the causes of potential abnormalities like this.[7]

Having known none of this at the time, the story took on something of an ethereal quality for me. The Japanese rail system was a force greater than the hard truth of physics, capable of superhuman feats to keep its rail systems running in near-perfect order. The reality is of course much more mundane but also more impressive. The knowledge that it isn't some mystical force that keeps the Japanese trains safe but rather the intense and rigorous layers of bureaucracy and regulation that result in such low incidents of accidents, rare cases of fatalities, and minimal inconvenience for everyone else availing themselves of the train system is the real magic of their trains. The only irony in this entire tale is that one train's 30 second delay managed to save 44 lives. I'm sure the operator that morning was frustrated by the delay, but ultimately, it was perhaps that lapse in bureaucratic perfection that saved lives. I think now that while there is a noble and worthwhile reason to pursue perfection (I say pursue not achieve intentionally), even bureaucratic perfection, sometimes it's those minor imperfections that create extra moments to let the happenstance wiggle its way into the picture and create opportunities for flukes of good fortune. So maybe the lesson is to strive for near not total perfection.

---

[7] Railway accident investigation report, Japan Transport Safety Board, published June 26, 2009 (https://www.mlit.go.jp/jtsb/eng-rail_report/English/RA2009-6-1e.pdf).

AINOTE

I made this ink and watercolor sketch from a photograph that I took of the wood carving of Kikazaru (hear not monkey), Mizaru (see not monkey), and Iwazaru (speak not monkey) that is carved on a wall of the Tōshō-gū Shrine at Rinnō-ji Temple in Nikkō, Japan in February 2008

> For when I close them,
> my eyes look beyond the here,
> to eternal peace.

Strangled on the wind—
our aspect branded in land,
the birds cry for you.

A face in the haze—
mist coalescing around,
obscuring my sight.

Golden bands of light;
wind whips voices to the void,
parting with the day.

To the distance, look—
a shadow moves against bright,
but you are not there.

Don't sit on your hands
and tell us that they are tied—
when we know better.

Fractional function—
broken but not completely,
golden painted lines.
The same words, the same—
the same shame, it's just the same—
the same lines, so lame.

Foundations of lies
cannot support the truth when
you try to tell it.

A fresh coat eases
the oppressive memory
of your betrayal.

Lurking beneath
the pretty words—left unsaid,
was venom in the heart.

Idalia, you bitch.
Had a date—you ruined it.

Vengeance will be mine.

DON'T BOTHER WITH TRANSLATION

So, I love the movie *Lost in Translation*. Friends and I even watched it while we were living in Tokyo huddled together on Carrie's bed in our Togoshi guesthouse. Sofia Coppola does an amazing job of gently picking apart that feeling of otherness that most *gaijin* feel when they first arrive in Tokyo and using it to tell a story of the unlikely romance born between drifting people isolated from themselves as much as from those around them. My only beef with the movie is that she uses, in some instances, inaccurate representations of Japan to create this atmosphere.

This happens repeatedly in the movie, such as during the hospital scene where the doctor just keeps explaining everything in Japanese without stopping. One example I always go back to is the *shabu-shabu* restaurant scene between the two main characters. ShabuZen, the restaurant where the scene was shot, which I've eaten at in both Tokyo and Kyoto, is nothing like the wretched quick-service style spread of raw beef presented in the movie. The Tokyo location is a gorgeous establishment in the basement of the Shibuya Creston Hotel. The restaurant itself is quite fancy, and the menus and attention to detail provided in the meal create a truly lovely experience. Unlike the *tabehodai* (all you can eat) *shabu-*

shabu joints in Shinjuku, where you really are left to your own devices, this restaurant is a destination, and I'm very sad that it was portrayed so flippantly in the movie. Mind you, I also love *tabehodai shabu-shabu*, and it's a great social meal when you want to be ultra-casual and just really hang out with friends.

Along with the concept of *tabehodai* is *nomihodai*, which means all you can drink. *Nomihodai*, like *tabehodai*, is based on a time limit, usually two hours. A lot of the *tabehodai shabu-shabu* restaurants also offer *nomihodai* packages. *Nomihodai* restaurants also have the interesting distinction of being very loud, even in reserved Japan. There must be something about the social knowledge that a large portion of the establishment's population is there to drink as much as they can in a short period of time.

My sister and I went with a large group of friends to one such *shabu-shabu* restaurant on the second floor of a building in Shibuya on my birthday to celebrate my senior citizen status among the group. Even with the usual fare of highly watered-down drinks served during *nomihodai*, we all managed to get loud and buzzed. My friend Patrick even got drunk enough that he ran around Shibuya and hugged every one of the "free hugs" folks milling about in the square. He grabbed one girl's sign from her and held it proudly above his head, upside down, offering hugs to passersby. I can't recall if he had any takers, but I snapped a photo of him proudly displaying the inverted sign for posterity. It might seem like we were a spectacle that night, but we were soundly upstaged by the *harajuku* girl who decided to sit in the middle of the sidewalk, legs splayed out in front of her, and weep loudly for the assembling crowd.[1] Her boyfriend bent over her trying to get her

---

[1] *Harajuku* girl refers to any Japanese woman who has dyed her hair white-blond, artificially tanned her skin, usually to a very orange result, and

to at least stand up and move out of the thoroughfare to no avail. Her loud wails continued even after we moved on down the street. My point is, if you're going to do *nomihodai*, make the most of the social pass you get for noise and raucous behavior.

Shabu-shabu, which translates to swish-swish in English, is a form of communal eating, such as fondue or hot pot in Korea. A pot of salted boiling water or vegetable broth is presented to a group of diners and kept simmering on a central burner set into the dining table. Platters of different cuts of meat in thin delicate slices and arrays of vegetables are also set out on the table. ShabuZen, in particular, takes this basic premise up a few notches. The restaurant provides a beautiful *kaiseki* (seasonal set menu which in its full glory is usually 10 to 12 small-bite courses) at the start before the *shabu-shabu* is brought to the table, each course in its own tiny plate with garnishes. *Sashimi,* spring onions and protein in a soy sauce aspic, and octopus dumpling with pink noodles under a paper-thin daikon flower were a few of the dishes my partner and I experienced as part of our ShabuZen *kaiseki*. A parade of textures and flavors. Each vessel, plate, bowl forms the lattice of a delicate garden with cobalt ceramic glaze, and intricate dishes in the shapes of leaves and flowers adorned with gold paint. A feast for the eyes as well as the palate. Just when you think your head might explode from the stimuli of the experience, the server brings the cooking vessel to the table, and at ShabuZen, it's an ornate and shining brass tureen hammered with designs around its edges and a wide base to catch spills.

---

wears skimpy, trendy clothes and giant heels. I don't say this to be derogatory. It isn't a slur. Like the girls who dress Lolita or Goth Lolita in Japan it is an actual fashion statement made by certain women.

Once the protein arrives, diners then pick up individual slices of raw meat with the thick ends of their chopsticks and swish it through the boiling water gently, so as to just cook the beef (or pork). Diners can also simmer the vegetables such as enoki mushrooms, bamboo shoots, and spring onions in the water to cook them as part of the dining experience. Little dishes of flavorful sauces are set before each person to dip the just cooked meat into before savoring it. The custom is to drop the meat into the small bowl of sauce and flip one's chopsticks to the eating side before raising the meat to the mouth. This keeps the communal bowl clean from germs but allows diners to use one set of chopsticks for eating. That is, if you're not with a giant group of drunk Americans having a birthday dinner. In that case, I'd expect to get some germs.

The entire experience is relaxed, leisurely, and pleasurable while maintaining that delicate but buttoned-up quality associated with fine dining in Tokyo. Traditional *shabu-shabu* also has a soup course, which ShabuZen provides for its diners as well. Once the meal has been consumed, the water that has now been cooking meats for an hour or more becomes the base for a soup. The server turns up the burner to bring the broth up to an intense boil. All remaining vegetables are tossed into the tureen to simmer. At a signal from the diners, the server will strain the broth into individual bowls with cooked noodles at the bottom, and this soup is shared by everyone at the table as a way to end the meal. It is such a gloriously efficient way to eat. One pot, multiple courses, no waste.

Absolutely none of the cultural intricacy, beautiful presentation, economy of dining, or anything else about *shabu-shabu* made it into the movie *Lost in Translation*. It was a thirty-second scene designed to bond the characters through a shared lack of understanding about Japanese culture. And that in a nutshell is why, although I loved the movie, I think there were parts where Sofia Coppola did Japan a disservice. Certainly, it is a valid argument that the characters were so desperately caught up in their own heads at this point in the movie that their lack of appreciation is on them not on the experience, but that might not be clear to the average movie-goer, particularly with the ridiculously obtuse, laminated picture menu that Bill Murray points to which is nothing like the actual menus at ShabuZen.

Perhaps a small point in Coppola's defense is that it is exceedingly hard to capture the feeling that any foreigner might have standing in a crowd and being utterly outside of it. And I know that's the feeling she was going for. The idea of being in a situation but also outside of that situation at the same time. So, from a cinematic standpoint, she probably had no choice if she wanted to convey a hard-to-understand feeling without experiencing it directly. So, maybe as someone who experienced it myself and also experienced many of the vignettes represented by the movie directly, I'm being overly critical. I still choose to be mildly offended on behalf of the restaurant ShabuZen and do recommend that if you are traveling to Japan, you experience *shabu-shabu* yourself in each of its incarnations.

ShabuZen aside, one particular experience Coppola presented accurately about Japan was *karaoke*. I will be the first to tell you that I'm not only a bad singer, but I'm pretty much tone deaf. Many, many years of singing alone in my car have perhaps allowed my ear to mirror—maybe memorize is the better word—the singing of others, but if I have no voice to follow along with, yikes! *Karaoke* in the United States, as of the early 2000s, was an exercise in horrific embarrassment for me. You would not have gotten me up in front of an entire bar of people to sing under any circumstance, monetary remuneration included. I think that other countries, including inside the United States, have started to adopt the atmosphere of Japanese *karaoke* in more recent years. If you have never had the opportunity to do *karaoke* Japanese-style, it is a marvelous experience. Since living in Japan, I've sung *karaoke* both inside and outside the United States, but I've never quite had the same experience as I did in Tokyo.

The Japanese make *karaoke* a private or friend-based experience. Sometimes individuals might show up to *karaoke* solo and can even be asked to be put in with an existing group, so as to avoid any minimum fees that might be charged to a solo singer. In the movie *Lost in Translation*, the scene is set in a large *karaoke* room with a little stage set up, and everyone takes their turns getting up to sing for their friends. At one point, the two main characters go out into the hallway and sit. This is essentially accurate to the experience, although the *karaoke* rooms we would visit in Gotanda were smaller with no chairs in the hallways. Each room is heavily soundproofed, so I didn't hear any meaningful noise from the people in the other rooms when we would walk through the hallways.

Instead of a stage, we all sat on a long bench that circled the entire room and enclosed a low table facing a TV that hung on the far wall next to the door. The table was covered in large books (although I assume it's now outfitted with iPads that let you select songs directly) containing massive lists of songs. Each song had a designated number, and all you needed to do to participate was find the number for the song you wanted to sing and punch it into the controller for the *karaoke* machine. Each room was also outfitted with not just one but a few microphones so that everyone could sing along to each song if they wanted. Each person in the group pre-pays for a couple of hours of *karaoke*, and the host or hostess shows you to your group's private room. Sometimes a set menu of drinks is included in the price, and sometimes it isn't. In the ancient days of 2008, there was a wall-phone set up in the room that would let you call down and order more drinks for the group.

That was it. It was a pretty simple set up. The song lists are vast, encompassing music from all areas of the world in all languages, current and classic. People just pick songs, enter them into the queue, and the television displays the lyrics and the audio system plays the music. It doesn't matter whether you can sing or not, because you're just among your friends, and our experiences of *karaoke* would quickly devolve into everyone singing all the songs, some into the microphones and some just yelling. *Karaoke* in Tokyo was one of the experiences that really helped me shed the social baggage connected to how I thought other people might perceive me. That's a convoluted way of saying that we often walk around letting what we think other people might be thinking about us dictate our actions in any given moment.

In my case, among others, the belief that people might think that I had no business holding a microphone up to my lips and singing out loud in front of everyone was one such perception. I still don't feel comfortable getting up in front of strangers and singing, but this group activity of putting all our talents or lack of same out there together and each person in turn accepting those talents or lack thereof with no judgment and only support helped me see that by not putting myself out there, I wasn't just avoiding negative reactions but was closing myself off from positive ones. Is it corny? Yes, it is. However, this fundamental shift in thinking gives someone with a lot of social anxiety like me a logical reason to risk the potential rejection since the reward of acceptance is an equally likely possibility.

I still remember vividly the most epic *karaoke* session we ever had. We were in our little room sucking down fruity alcoholic drinks with some of the guys drinking straight *shochu* (like vodka but made from rice). We were perhaps only half an hour into our session when our wall phone rang.

"Hello," said Patrick, answering the phone. He listened for a couple of seconds, said OK, and then set the phone back on the wall. "There's a Japanese guy by himself, and he wanted to be with a group. They asked if he could join our room. I said sure."

We all looked at each other and shrugged. This was the first time a stranger wanted to *karaoke* with us. A minute or two later, a skinny Japanese man with full head of messy black hair entered the room with a slight bow. He was a salary man probably in his late 30s or early 40s wearing the standard uniform of a black suit, white shirt, and skinny black tie. He didn't speak much English, and I don't remember if he even told us his name, but I will call him Kohei for the sake of this story. Kohei was the name of one of my classmates' Japanese boyfriend at the time. Neither she nor her Kohei were there that night. Our new friend Kohei took a seat and began leafing through the books, and we all just continued as we were picking songs and putting them on the list. We went about our usually loud, group singing. There was little skill involved but a lot of gregarious ribbing and drama. Kohei didn't speak to us, but he smiled, nodded, and bopped along to our song choices. In the entirely inscrutable way of the Japanese, I can't tell if he was actually enjoying himself, but it seemed that way to me.

Perhaps forty-five minutes or so later, a song started up that none of us recognized. We all froze for a minute, looking confused until Kohei stood up and gestured for the mic, which Houston handed him. The unfamiliar music transitioned into an intense beat, and Kohei proceeded to then rap his ever-loving heart out to a completely boggling Japanese rap song. With his jacket off and tie flying, Kohei threw down hard while all of us stood there gob smacked. I finally recovered from my stupor enough to pull out my camera phone and record a video of the *karaoke* screen.[2] When the hard beat finally subsided, Kohei handed the microphone back to Houston as the other guys circled him to smack him on the back or give him high fives. Once the accolades had subsided, he picked up his jacket, tucked it over his arm, gave us all another short, stiff bow and a sly grin and departed without another word. We all lost our collective shit after that, howling at each other in glee and marveling at the speed of the rap lyrics. I wonder sometimes that we didn't chase Kohei down and get his information to invite him to future *karaoke* nights, but he didn't speak English, and we didn't speak enough Japanese, and sometimes life just happens such that you meet people in a way that you will remember them forever even if you don't know their name or anything about their life. And the impression of the experience and elation that comes with strong emotion imprints your soul, even if you can never tell the person how they made you feel in that moment.

It might just be, despite Sofia Coppola's attempts at bringing the oddness and wonder of Japanese culture to Americans, some experiences are just better off not translated.

---

[2] If I hadn't gone back and looked at that video and then googled some of the lyrics, I wouldn't even be able to tell you who the artist was or what the song was, because it was incomprehensibly fast. If you are a fan of Japanese rap music, however, the song was *Ningen Hatsudenjo* which translates to Human Power Plant in English by the artist Buddha Brand. I recognized the song by the lyrics "keep fresh Buddha" flying across the screen in English.

AINOTE

I made this ink and watercolor sketch from a photograph I took during the Makuuchi (highest rank of sumo) Entrance Ceremony at the Sumo Grand Tournament in January 2008

        Flames lick at a branch,
        illuminating faces—
          then a susurrus.

        Gliding silk slips
   through rough fingers—lingering
     on the edge, torn away.

Fabric swirls on calves—
swishing movement as we amble
past that last bleached dune.

Flames lick the old shed
that stores memories of you,
burned beyond knowing.

Curled in on itself,
the perfumed scent of summer
wafts across me—prone.

Watching love die slow—
withering fruit on the vine,
giving naught to none.

Crumpled feelings ache
below my lungs—breathe in, out
ripping through the spine.

By moonlight—squinting
thoughts flit sad on broken wings;
desertion complete.

A LABIA-SCALDING NIGHT ON THE TOWN

When I first arrived in Tokyo, apart from being horribly ill from the aforementioned kidney infection, I vowed unequivocally that I would in no way shape or form get naked in a large pool of water with a bunch of strangers. If you're confused, this practice is called taking *onsen* (a natural hot spring) or *sentō* (Japanese public bath). It's an extremely common pastime and an elaborate process that results in ample naked time with a plethora of total strangers, an activity that is lauded as highly relaxing. I was not on board.

While living in Tokyo, there wasn't much that I didn't try out. I ate any number of creatures (horse, whale—both raw, of course—and even a horde of tiny fish that looked like white worms with little black eyeballs called *shirasu* which are actually super yummy).[1]

---

[1] Regarding the whale meat, I didn't order it. It came as part of a *kaiseki* (a formal dinner comprised of ten to twelve tiny courses of seasonally available food) at a *ryokan* (traditional Japanese inn) that I was staying at on my spring break trip to Kyoto. The lovely young lady serving the meal explained each dish to us, but when she got to the tiny cup of white cubes, she couldn't remember the word in English. "*Kagura, Kagura*", she said, scrunching up her face in concentration and dragging out the word. I knew I had heard the word before, but I could not remember what *kagura* meant. Finally, she began to

I visited M's Pop Life adult department store, a seven-story sex toy and pornography shop in Akihabara. I spent a couple hours in a love hotel with my partner at the time. Some girlfriends and I even tried out a maid cafe, although it was an underwhelming experience since the entire vibe and included activities were very much catered to lonely young men. The "maids" got more out of it than we did. They were highly entertained that a few female *gaijin* came to visit and eat ice cream sundaes, and they gave us lots of attention and asked us questions, much to the chagrin of the men there for female attention.

Even with all of that, *onsen* was one part of immersing myself in another culture that I initially wouldn't even consider. In my mind, I had really good reasons for resisting the persistent claims of my classmates that it was amazing, so relaxing, and basically the best thing ever. Apart from the *gaijin* factor, which is an issue for any foreigner living in Japan, there was the added twist that only a couple years earlier I had lost 125 pounds of body mass. This added, both emotionally and practically, to my feeling ill at ease with public nudity.

When you lose 125 pounds of weight, there are just a couple of cold, hard facts on the other side. One, your skin probably isn't going to bounce back, particularly if you have stretch marks and are

---

pantomime an animal by making a little spout of water shoot out of her head with her fingers and saying "pewwwwwwww pewwwwwwwww" until I exclaimed "Whale!" "Ahhhh," she replied, nodding and smiling. Ultimately, it was too hilarious to negate her efforts and I didn't want to waste food that was provided by our hosts, so I ate the whale. If you were wondering, it was oddly crunchy and mostly tasteless. It was by no means something I enjoyed eating, and even if I did, I wouldn't order it on principle alone because of Japan's controversial whale-fishing practices, but I don't regret the experience of trying it when provided.

over a certain age. It just won't. Two, even if you are lucky enough to have a plastic surgeon for a father, as I am, and can get thousands of dollars of surgery for free, you will not be perfect. There will be scars, big ones. There will be floppy bits, large patches of cellulite leftover from connective tissue loosened from weight loss, and skin that doesn't quite hang right. There will be leftover stretch marks. It's just the reality of massive weight loss.

I began gaining weight around age nine, when my parents separated. I struggled with my weight all through middle and high school, but after college, the struggle became a war that I was losing. I ultimately topped out at 255 pounds on a 5'3" frame. Frankly, though, that may not even have been my top weight. I refused to weigh myself for a while at the point that I was wearing size 24 pants. Therapy and hard work on my mental health and anxiety fixed my reasons for eating but not my weight. Ultimately, the year before I started law school, in October 2005, my grandmother and my mother gave me the immense gift of paying for the lap-band procedure for me.

The procedure was relatively new and not yet covered by any insurance policy. Out of pocket, it was $14,000 and to this day, they both think it is the best money they ever spent. I can't disagree. It changed my life in ways that are hard to describe. If you've never been obese, you can't understand what it feels like to be ignored as you walk through life. If you've only been heavy, you can't understand how truly different you are treated by people for something that often you can't do much about. I can, however, tell you the exact day that I became socially acceptable.

Right after my surgery, when I would eat out at restaurants and not finish my food, the waiter or waitress would ask, "Did you not like the food?" or "Was there a problem?" or "Is everything OK?" Without fail, this was always the question. Left unsaid was assumption that a fat person like me would in no way leave food on her plate for any other reason. One day, perhaps six months into my weight loss, the waiter said these life-changing words: "Do you want a box?"

That simple act of asking if I wanted a box rather than assuming I didn't like the food blew my mind. That feeling branded itself into my consciousness. That day was the day that I became a socially acceptable size. When I was at my smallest, they started asking me if I wanted a box before I'd even finished eating, assuming that someone who's 118 lbs doesn't eat food anyway. It wasn't the only way people changed their behavior toward me, but it profoundly affected me, and I still think about it. As a child, I never had anyone to look up to and feel OK about my body. There were no fat pop stars when I was young.

So, in 2008, as a newly minted women's size 4 still acclimating to feeling like I looked like the socially acceptable pretty girl, I wasn't eager to expose the raw underbelly (or any kind of belly really) of the less palatable side of my weight loss. At the end of the day, I still had it miles better than the lovely pre-op trans woman in my class who wasn't able to enjoy *onsen* openly, so looking back, I shouldn't have been such a baby about it. There is always someone struggling more.

Fast forward a couple of months into the semester, and my friend Olivia was wearing me down with her glowing descriptions of *onsen*.

"It's only other women.

No one looks at you.

You can't understand how relaxing it is.

There's nothing better on a cold night.

Just come with us this one time. You won't regret it."

I'm still not sure which argument actually swayed me. It is funny how peer pressure works, in every conceivable way. FOMO and the fear of being rejected by my friends because I'm lame for not engaging in public bathing ended up being somehow worse than displaying the facts of weight loss to a bunch of strangers and a few close friends. To this day, I can't reasonably explain why I let it all hang out, in the most literal sense, but I did, and doing that helped me drop the mental weight that I didn't even realize I was still lugging around. It was suddenly acceptable to me in my own mind to have the battle scars of weight loss etched on my body.

My first experience taking *onsen* was at an actual *onsen* theme park. Yes, that's right. It was a theme park that was a collection of natural spring baths, one side for women and the other for men, and between the two sections was a food court and market where you could hang out and get ramen, ice cream, and shop for knickknacks all in the theme of an old Edo (Edo being the original name of Tokyo) street in Japan. It was called Odaiba Oedo Onsen Monogatari. It sadly closed down permanently in 2021 after being open for almost twenty years due to the lease for the facility expiring. If you are ever in the Odaiba section of Tokyo, perhaps see if it has sprung up somewhere new. In 2008, it was a place you could stay overnight by just finding a corner to sleep in when you were tired. ¥2000 ($20) got you in until before the last train and ¥3000 ($30) let you stay overnight until the next day when the trains started running again. In any event, Olivia finally convinced me to try taking *onsen* at Odaiba, and it was everything she said and more!

Wait, you are thinking. *What about the labia-scalding part?* I promise, I'll get to it.

On the evening I relented, a group of us took the Yurikamome Line out to Odaiba, paid our yen, and were given a wrist key to a locker. The key had a tag on it that let us charge anything we wanted to buy in the shops to our locker number, and we could then settle our charges as we left the park. This mercifully obviated the need to carry cash around inside the bath areas. From there, we went to a locker room and changed into bathing *yukata* (light kimono robes) provided by the *onsen*. Completely unencumbered and naked except for our *yukata* and wrist key, we wandered around for a bit browsing the small shops and checking out the food options. This area of the park was co-ed, and so we were able to grab a bowl of ramen with the guys from our group or utilize the co-ed foot baths, but when it was time to finally making our way to the baths, women went to the left and men went to the right, each having an entirely separate set of baths at our disposal, each accessible through a solid door. The baths themselves were impressively magnificent.

For the unfamiliar, Japanese public bathing is a very specific process. All persons wishing to soak in a spring or bath must first engage in a rigorous public scrubbing. Stools are set up along areas lined with a series of open stalls, each having a spigot and hose for washing. Odaiba was fancier than most, so there were mirrors and bottles of shampoo and other cleansers set out. Olivia and I each grabbed a stool and disrobed to wash. The only cloth allowed in the bathing area is a washcloth and a tea towel, both provided by the *onsen*. No bathing suits are allowed in *onsen* or *sentō* as they are considered unsanitary. Instead, the tea towel is there to provide modesty, although who's I'm not sure, as it barely covered one of my DD breasts. We soaped up and vigorously cleaned every inch of ourselves at our own stations, using the provided spray hoses to spray off the soap and dirt. Body, hair, face, everything squeaky clean. From there, we took our now pretty wet modesty towels and thoroughly clean bodies and wandered into the baths, which consisted of ten or more well-appointed pools at temperatures varying from hot to intensely hot. Some had jets for massage. Some were inside in a giant hall. Some were outside. Some were shallow and relaxing, others deep. Imagine every conceivable type of jacuzzi, and that was what Odaiba Onsen Monogatari was like. You just moved from pool to pool and soaked in the different temperatures.

We were supposed to alternate in and out, warm and hot, because it's very easy to pass out spending too much time in the hot water. I almost did at least twice, finally picking up a bottle of cold water from a vending machine with my handy wrist key to carry around the tubs. Somehow, walking to a vending machine naked actually felt more naked than doing any of these other nude activities that I'd already been doing for a half hour.

My favorite pool was the outdoor one. It was still quite cold out at night in March, so being in the outdoor *onsen* was like riding around in a convertible in the winter. Your head was nice and cool, but your body was hot and relaxed. It was heaven. So, what does this have to do with my lady parts getting burned? Nothing, actually! This is the counterpoint, my lovelies. This is the high end, up-scale theme park experience of *onsen*.

Sentō, however. *Sentō* is local. *Sentō* can be nice, or it can be gritty. *Sentō* is the 80-year-old woman in a lifeguard chair yelling at you to get to your respective area of the plastic divider side of public bathing. That's the side you see when it's nine at night, cold as fuck out, your classes just ended, and a group of you decides to take a quick *sentō* in an off-the-beaten-path neighborhood before heading home. That's the side of Japanese public bathing that will burn you and your labia.

A group of six of us, three guys and three girls decided to partake of our local *sentō* on one such frigidly cold March evening. It was within walking distance of our school located in the Mita section of Tokyo. We followed along after Evan, who'd swore that he loved this *sentō* and went there all the time. Evan was a seasoned Japanophile, spoke and read a decent amount of the language, and was responsible for more than one interesting experience at a local dive establishment.[2] We wound our way through dark streets, past

---

[2] For our first group meal of the semester, not counting the school-hosted welcome dinner, Evan guided us to a tiny hole-in-the-wall restaurant, the name of which was just the kanji symbol for *tori* (chicken). And it was just that, in fact. Chicken on a stick. Any part of the chicken you might want to try, you could get it on a stick. Livers, hearts, cartilage, and tendons even—it was all available grilled on a skewer. Or not grilled, even. One of the options was "seared" chicken breast, which I did not partake of, as I felt like raw chicken would have been absolutely begging my still-recovering body to revolt on me again. The restaurant was very small, and there were probably eight of us, so the staff directed us to a separate room in the back where we all squeezed into a booth around a table on the ground, and Evan deciphered the menu for us. We ordered lots of bizarre cuts of chicken, even the seared skewers, and a whole lot of beer. At one point, Houston had to empty his bladder and was directed to a tiny room next to ours. He was in there a really, really long time. We began to ask ourselves if someone shouldn't go check on him, but none of us really wanted to. Who knew what intestinal gymnastics he was dealing with. When he eventually did emerge, his face red from exertion or embarrassment, not sure which, he regaled us with his experience using the Japanese-style toilet, the only one available in the restaurant. It apparently took him multiple attempts to figure out how to utilize the facility, because in his drunken state, he was concerned about falling into the bowl. I am familiar with how men urinate. It doesn't usually require any special gymnastic ability to accomplish, but Houston swore to us that the only way that he would be able to use the toilet was to completely remove his pants and underwear, which he apparently did. I didn't want to speculate too hard on the necessary activities, but he apparently then needed to find a place to set both his trousers and underpants, which was also a trial. You could have sworn the experience was a full-blown reenactment of The Tale of Genji. By the end, none of us could contain our laughter, and to this day, I'm still not

small buildings set into quiet neighbors and arrived at a red *sentō* sign. With almost no other discernible features to indicate that this was a bath, it was apparent that this *sentō* was nothing like Odaiba Onsen Monogatari, which was to be expected, for sure. But honestly, this *sentō* was extremely basic, even for a *sentō*. I've seen plenty of photos of other *sentō* online, and this one was the Waffle House of *sentō*. We were there for the local experience, though, so we just went for it.

Through the tiled entry and into the main room was a quick walk, barely past one set of glass doors. Modesty was secondary to utility. After handing the meager ¥470 to the old lady manning the booth, the guys were directed to the right, past the old lady who had an ample view into both sides of the facility. Olivia, Becca, and I were directed to the left. The only other women on our side that evening were two elderly ladies up to their chins in the heavily steaming water and two teenage girls, who were chatting with each other at the far end of the pool.

As usual, we tried to avert our eyes and go about our business cleaning ourselves. This *sentō* didn't provide fancy things like free soaps and shampoo, so we grabbed some from a vending machine near the door and set to work. After taking the time to do the thorough scrub, Becca, Olivia and I moved to the edge of the pool to sink into the hot water. That was the plan, anyway… but, holy shit! The water wasn't just hot. It was scalding, searing, boiling. It was organ-poaching. I stepped onto a stair and almost screamed. All contrived social niceties of averting eyes and pretending we weren't a bunch of women naked together in a public pool was scorched away in one fell swoop, along with the skin on my foot.

---

sure what happened in that toilet, and I wouldn't be surprised if Houston isn't either.

All eyes were now on us. It wasn't just me. Becca's entire face turned purple trying to navigate into the pool. Olivia looked unsettlingly blotchy. We gave each other frantic looks as we tried to inch our respective ways into the water.

"We'll acclimate," Becca said.

"It'll just be a minute," I agreed.

"Or maybe five," Olivia added.

As we moved lower, and lower, slowly, into the water, I could see that the gazes of the elderly women were sparkling with laughter. It was like we were animals entertaining the locals at the zoo. We tried to make small talk, pretending we weren't sitting there completely butt and everything else naked on the side of the pool trying to maneuver into it without screaming bloody murder.

"You have nice breasts," I finally said to Becca at one point.

"Yours are really great," she replied.

Whatever modesty we'd been able to feign through our collective *onsen* and *sentō* experiences to date was a polite social contract that had been just torn to shreds. Lumpy thighs, scars, and stretch marks all bared and in places angry red for everyone to see.

"Thanks," I replied. "My dad did them."

I hoped to hell those Japanese ladies didn't speak English. We just kept pushing ourselves into the water as best we could. Every eye in that bath was firmly fixed on us in direct contravention to all expectation of Japanese manners. The older ladies were even snickering at us. All semblance of dignity had fled the *sentō*.

With time ticking by and my body not getting any more relaxed, I finally, with one last determined bout of effort, pushed my thighs into the water and slid lower. The moment that scalding-hot water hit my labia, I yelled.

"Nope! No fucking way! I'm out!"

I abandoned ship with a less than graceful splash, gritting my teeth as the scalding water erupted upward into my already-abused vulva, the ladies guffawing and clapping. For a country that eats half their food raw, I didn't see the point in hard-boiling themselves, but that's an entirely different story. I might have been the first one out of the pool, but Becca and Olivia quickly followed. Already denied my hot soak in a tub, I was grumpy, and I patently refused to go out into the cold air with a wet head of hair. This neighborhood *sentō* didn't provide hair dryers at the open stalls, but it did have one of those old heat helmet chairs that salons have. My hair was short, an overgrown shag that didn't even touch my shoulders, so I had no problem sticking my head under that heated helmet, inserting my yen into the slot and letting it blow my hair around into a giant fauxhawk. At least I wasn't walking out into the cold with a dripping wet head. Becca and Olivia laughed as the hair whipped around my face, but I had zero fucks to give at that point. We all laughed.

Olivia was a different story, though. She had long, fine blond hair that fell well past her shoulders and down her back. When she sat down into that chair and flipped it on, we all gritted our teeth, wavering between laughing and crying, as it blew her hair into a gigantic, spiraled tangle of yellow-blond. By now the teenage girls who had been silently enjoying our antics from a distance closed in. They were fascinated by Olivia's cyclone of hair, and as we finally made our way out of the ragged little *sentō* with its lava-filled pool, head hair tangled into avant garde shapes, a backward glance caught the teenagers videotaping each other on their camera phones as their hair whipped about under the salon helmet, old ladies smirking in the corner.

"That was so relaxing," said Evan as we walked out into the brisk night, coats pulled up around our necks.

I exchanged a look with Becca, and we held in yet another giggle.

"Your side wasn't too hot?" Olivia asked.

"No, why? What happened to your hair?" he asked her.

We busted out laughing, and the guys all gave as an odd look as we just walked on towards the train station. That was the last time we were taking Evan's advice on a *sentō*.

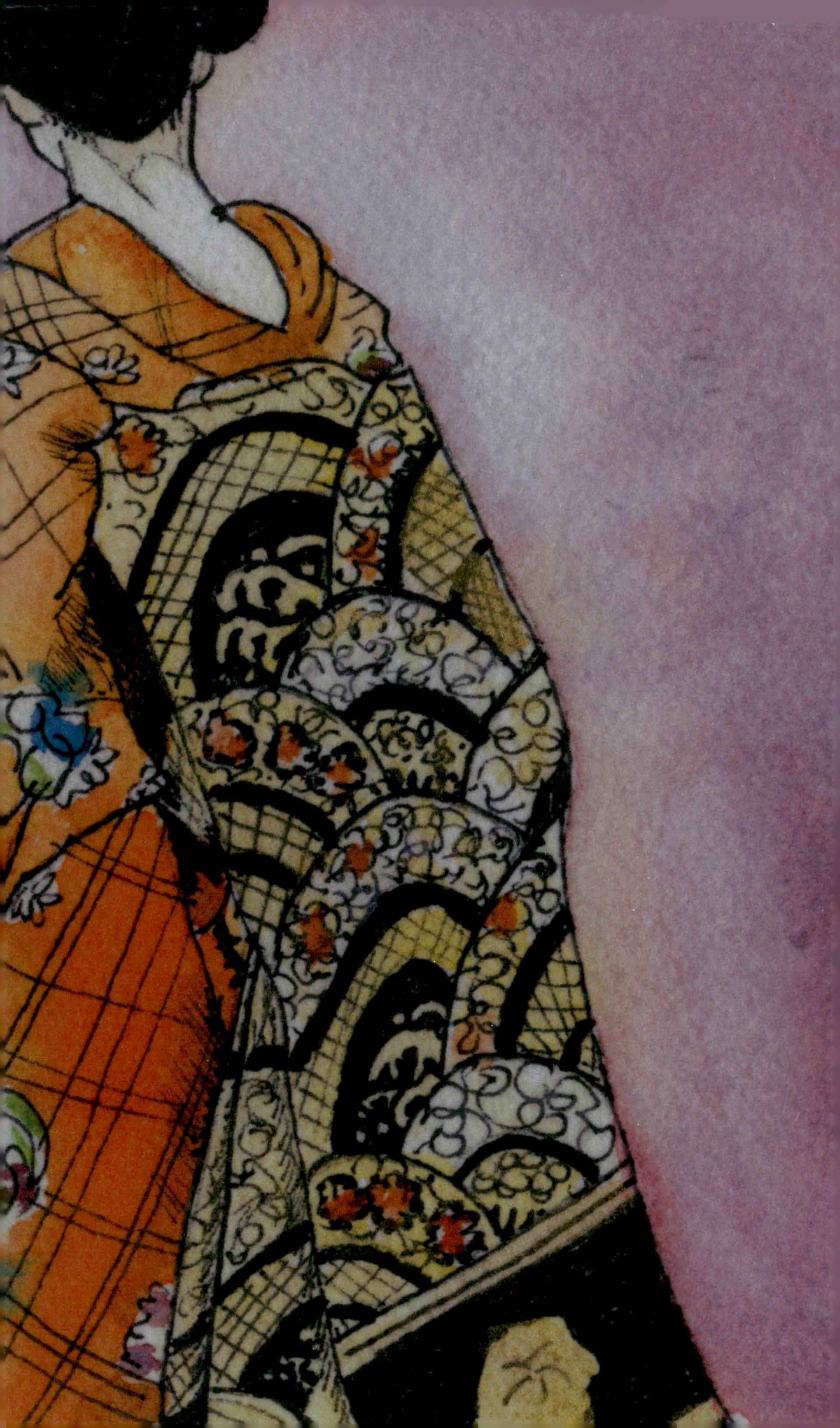

AINOTE

I made this ink and watercolor sketch from a photograph I took of Maiko Fumitama in March of 2008, as she hurried past me in Gion, Kyoto. Maiko are geisha in training.

Almost orgasmed
as you whispered in my ear,
"Meet me in St Lucia."

Sleepless—pondering
the scent of you in my sheets,
and I can't forget.

Surrender to me
on a silken bed of grass,
as rain beats down hard.

On my stereo,
Spectacular Rival plays—
love you 'till the end.

The rain crashes as
we lay together, silent.
The world outside weeps.

Your body on mine.
Find that place—reckless heat,
winter night warmer.

Conjured in my mind—
the image of your body
beneath my hips, rocking.

In the dark—soft lips
whispering need, fingers clash,
grasping to forget.

I gave so freely
of my mind, body, and love—
an error undone.

Beneath dripping blooms,
your lips find my collarbone—
deft fingers explore.

Soft light flickering
over golden skin, exposed,
lit from within—charged.

Soft breath strokes my ear—
sending tickles down my spine.
Exposed but secret.

YAKUZA-A-GO-GO

My favorite professor at Temple University Japan (TUJ) was Professor Matthew Wilson. He used to practice at the first law firm and even in the office that I worked for after law school. He had long since moved on to academia by 2008, but the litigators at my old firm still remembered him fondly, and I am convinced that knowing him helped my resume get noticed. I had originally contacted Professor Wilson before I even applied to law school to ask about TUJ's semester in Tokyo and got to know him before I even applied to the firm. By the time I arrived in Japan, I had emailed with, spoken to, and even met my Japanese Law professor in Florida. He would travel around the country speaking about TUJ, and I had the opportunity to greet him when he came to my regular old law school, the University of Florida. I say all of this because Professor Wilson was a critical component to all of us having a successful semester in Tokyo. I was very glad to hear that, as of 2020, he is back at TUJ as the Dean for the entire campus. There is not a single other person I would want to be there if I had a crisis in Tokyo. I would pick him over my mom in that specific instance! Between the time I was at TUJ in 2008 and 2020, he moved back to the United States for several years to support his son, James, and help him achieve the dream of becoming a world class pianist. James realized that dream, even playing the Kennedy

Center at age nine and Carnegie Hall for the first time as an eleven-year-old. Professor Wilson cares deeply about his family, and he treats his students like family.

When we were under his care in Tokyo, he was the mother duck. He took Becky to the hospital when she had unknowingly eaten raw pork that was meant for *shabu-shabu* and developed an intestinal infection. And then he took her back when the infection didn't clear the first time. He was always ready with a kind and understanding word, recommendations, or advice, and he taught us an incredible amount of not just Japanese law but also Japanese culture. He was also a great resource for students who wanted to work in Tokyo, being in 2008 one of the only recognized *gaiben* (foreign *bengoshi*) in Japan. With blond hair, blue eyes, and a ready smile, it was and probably still is disturbing to many Japanese lawyers and businessmen how well he speaks their language and understands their culture.

One of the most critical speeches he gave early on in our tenure at TUJ was about the *yakuza* (gangsters). Pretty much all of us had heard of the *yakuza* before, and we had some interesting lessons about them and their interactions with the Japanese legal system as part of our Japanese Law class, but Professor Wilson was most interested in helping his students avoid run-ins with the *yakuza* in their daily lives.

"I urge you to all be careful in Roppongi," he would say.[1] "Let me tell you a story. A few years ago, we had a student who went

---

[1] Roppongi is another district inside Minato, where our school was located. It's known for having an affluent area and a large nightclub scene. Because there are a lot of foreign embassies in the district as well, there are a lot of foreigners from Africa, Russia and other parts of the world that work in the nightclubs as bartenders, bouncers, and women hired to drug men. On the

into a Roppongi bar one night. He sat down at the bar and was quickly approached by two beautiful women. They were foreign women, not Japanese. He brought them drinks and they all got to chatting."

He paused for effect.

"When he was good and drunk, one of them turned to him and said, 'We know a great private bar, where we can really have a party. Let us take you.'"

"So, this student left with the women. They walked for a bit through a maze of small streets, and the student was already quite drunk. When they got the bar, it was empty except for the

---

few times I would walk through Roppongi, I would be accosted repeatedly by very large men begging me to come into their clubs as I would walk down the street. Sometimes they would even try to take me by the shoulder and physically direct me into their club. I wasn't having any of that, but it was some of the only times I ever felt uneasy walking in Tokyo. Starting with the opening of Roppongi Hills and the Roppongi Tower in the early 2000s, portions of Roppongi had already begun to change while I was there. The nightclub scene has continued to grow even larger, with a wide range of nightclubs and shows, including strip clubs, hostess clubs, cabarets, drag shows, and other various entertainment. Since my class left Tokyo, however, it seems as if the *yakuza* has lost some of its hold on Roppongi. For instance, the building of the company Toa Soko Kigyo, which was a front of the Toseikai *yakuza* gang was vacated in 2008 not long after we left Japan, through a convoluted property rights dispute that resulted in the explosion and demolition of a few of the clubs in that building. Roppongi is not all bad, and some of my classmates absolutely loved to go there. I saw an amazing, artistic drag show there that my sister was very keen to experience called Roppongi Kinyo, which I describe further in my essay "Roppongi Redux". It was fantastic, and many of the performers were transitioning women rather than drag queens. The costumes, set design, performance, and atmosphere was mind-boggling. Even families would come to this show to celebrate birthdays, and we saw groups of all size and age enjoying this entertainment.

bartender. From there, everything was a blank. The next thing the student knew, he was waking up in the street."

The students shared uneasy looks.

"His wallet, which had contained his rent money in cash for the coming month, was empty. What do you think the lesson is there?" He asked.

"Don't carry a lot of cash to bars," one student responded.

"Yes, that's a really good point," Professor Wilson said, "and when I told that story the year after to the next class, that was what I advised."

"But then," he said, giving another slightly dramatic pause, "I had another student go out to Roppongi." Professor Wilson was a skillful lecturer, and he had us all on the edge of our seats.

"Well, did he take cash again?" someone else asked, unable to completely hide his mild amusement at this parade of what I guess he considered idiots.

"No," said Professor Wilson. "He thought he would be smart and only bring a few thousand yen (the rough equivalent of $20-40) with him to go out. Again, this young man woke up after having been drugged. And the next time he checked his bank balance, it showed that he or possibly someone else had withdrawn ¥300,000 ($3,000) from his bank account. His debit card was still with him. Of course, he had no idea who were the ladies he was drinking with, where he'd been or what happened. Everyone was long gone by then."

"Okay," someone chimed in, "So no cash and leave all your cards at home." Some of the male students were eager to get concrete and very specific safety advice that they could use. We were going to be lawyers, after all.

"Well," said Professor Wilson, his look becoming even more serious. "You might be able to guess what happened next. The next year, I told both of these stories just as I'm telling them to you, and the students swore they would be careful."

"But, inevitably, one student went to Roppongi. He left all his cards at home except a small amount of cash and his ID." [2]

"Well, what could they possibly do with that?" the indignant student asked.

Professor Wilson gave each of us a grave look, but there was a glint in his eye.

"This young man woke up at home not remembering anything at all that had happened the night before. He was initially relieved, thinking he'd managed to escape any danger. But then, there was a knock on his door."

---

[2] As a side note, in 2008, foreigners were required to carry either their passport or their Japanese government-issued identification card at all times. If you are stopped by the Metropolitan Police as a *gaijin* and are not carrying identification, you are very likely to be arrested, particularly if you are riding a bike, which a lot of us did to get around between school and home. So, everyone always carried their Japanese ID cards. Carrying our ID cards and how to avoid getting arrested was an entirely different speech from Professor Wilson. I can't confirm that this is still the case in present day, but in 2008, approximately 90% of the population of Fuchu Prison, the largest prison in Japan was foreigners of some type. It is a maximum-security facility, but all foreign prisoners are detained at Fuchu. Our class visited Fuchu, but I was ill that day and could not drag myself out of bed to attend, which really bummed me out. Fuchu Prison houses the men, but if I had been arrested, I would have been sent to Tochigi Prison, located in a rural area north of Tokyo, and instead of learning carpentry or mechanics, they would have taught me to be a beautician or a seamstress. So, yeah… not completely misogynistic or anything.

Everyone's eyes went wide. It began to feel like a ghost story told around the campfire. I suddenly wanted popcorn. Professor Wilson continued.

"The student answered the door and found two men there. They pushed their way into his apartment and informed him that he had a bar tab of ¥600,000 ($6,000), a truly astronomical amount, and that they were coming to collect the money owed. The student was terrified. They had looked at his ID while he was drugged, and they now knew where he lived."

You could have heard a camel bat an eyelash in the room at that moment.

"To get them to leave, he gave them all the cash he had in the apartment and his credit card. From there, he came to me."

Professor Wilson gave each student a look again.

"We had to cancel the card and find him another apartment to live in before the *yakuza* came back to ask him why the card didn't work. He spent the rest of the semester looking over his shoulder."

Looking around the room, everyone was open-mouthed in shock.

"The point," said Professor Wilson continued, as if he was arguing a point of fact before the Supreme Court of the United States, "is that it doesn't matter how safe you think you are being, when you go to bars in Roppongi, they have the upper hand. They own the bars. The women are hired to get you drunk, the bartenders work for them and won't hesitate to drug and leverage you, and they are creative and ruthless. I can't keep you from going to Roppongi, but every year I have a story like this."

He let that statement hang in the air for a moment, forcing every guy in the class to steep in the fact that he expected one of them to be the next cautionary tale. And it was sobering to many of us. Did it stop everyone from visiting Roppongi? No, definitely not. Did I hear about any run-ins with the *yakuza* by any of my classmates? Also, no. You can imagine my surprise, then, when I actually did see real life *yakuza* while wondering around a quiet street in Kyoto Gion during my spring break.

I am by no means an expert on the Japanese criminal and political world, but to a certain extent, my understanding is that, historically, the police in Japan have had a quasi-symbiotic relationship with the *yakuza* groups. It isn't as clear-cut as there being good cops and bad cops. It is more like a delicate cultural dance that results in certain activities being ignored until such time as the government can get creative and bring charges, or better yet, dispense the issue with no police involvement of any kind. Part of this is a function of the Japanese legal system and the culture of the Metropolitan Police in Japan not bringing a case until they are certain they will be able to convict. There's a reason why the conviction rate in Japan is 99.9%.

It is a circle that starts with taking cases likely to be convicted, leveraging the conviction rate to build trust, and then using the trust as a basis for a presumed guilty mentality. It's a self-fulfilling prophecy in some ways. The Japanese police take cases that they can make iron-clad and through these actions build immense trust in their skills as officers of the law, which makes the courts show deference to the police to a greater degree than we see in the United States. They also rely heavily on confessions, which generally would be a good indicator of guilt, except when those confessions are obtained through threats or other means that cast doubt on their veracity. This veracity is often not questioned, however, because of the reputation that the Japanese police have built within their communities.

This is not me bashing the Japanese police or courts. To a large degree, I believe that the deeply rooted cultural need for consensus within any social, corporate, or political structure inside Japan is a primary motivator of this trust and coordination. Additionally, pressing hard for a confession in and of itself indicates a need to seek consensus, even with the offender. It would be uncomfortable for most Japanese people to take any serious action without this consensus, particularly given the complex relationship between hierarchy, honor, shame, and forgiveness that has been part of Japan's culture for thousands of years. To ask the average person, even a police officer, to go with their gut and inconvenience others by taking a stance contrary to the group, defend that stance publicly, and then challenge the beliefs of others, even if their own belief is strongly held would be like trying to plant a water lily in the desert.[3] In any event, this complex relationship between gangster and government resulted in the locals knowing their friendly, neighborhood *yakuza* boss.

While on spring break in Kyoto, my friend Amey and I decided to book a walking tour of the *ochiya* (tea houses) of Gion, a historic area in Kyoto where the *maiko* (*geiko* in training) and *geiko* (the word for *geisha* in the Kyoto dialect) still work today.[4]

---

[3] Unless you're talking about a water lily in the Bosten Lake, in Xinjiang, China, which is surrounded by the Gobi Desert, in which case, this action is totally reasonable.

[4] If you look at the painting immediately preceding this essay, you will see the back of a *maiko*. I painted this from a photograph that I took during the Gion walking tour referenced here. You can tell she is a *maiko* based on her *obi* (belt). We were extremely lucky during our walk and passed multiple *maiko* and *geiko* hurrying about their business that afternoon. There a few quick ways to spot the difference between a *maiko* and a *geiko*. One, the *maiko* will wear a *furisode*, a type of *kimono* with very long sleeves that hang almost

The tour was conducted by a *gaijin* who had been living in Gion for twenty years. He was tanned and sandy blond but wore the hell out of an earth-toned *yukata* (casual summer kimono), maybe in an effort to minimize the fact that we were all *gaijin* flouncing around a quiet historic neighborhood. He made his living doing tours, and that day, Amey and I were the only ones, so we spent a pleasant couple of hours wandering around Gion at a leisurely pace, learning about the famous *ochiya* and furtively *geisha*-spotting.

We got very lucky and saw a couple of *maiko* and one *geiko* fully decked out in their makeup and finery hurrying about their business before the evening performances were to begin, but the completely unexpected find was the stick-thin man in his eighties casually strolling the street towards us in a periwinkle, velour

---

to the ground, while the *geiko* will wear shorter sleeves. *Furisode* are traditionally worn by unmarried girls in Japan, so this makes sense from a cultural perspective, since the *maiko* has not yet reached maturity in her skills and licensure, which requires five years of training. Two, the *maiko* will wear a *darari obi*, which hangs down much lower than the *geiko obi*, which is folded and tucked into a bun on the *geiko's* back. Also, the *maiko*'s *obi* features the crest of the *okiya* (another word for tea house) where they are affiliated during their training (this would be hidden if the *obi* was folded). Three, the *maiko* will sport a thin, red collar on her *kimono*, and the *geiko's* collar will be white. And, finally, the *maiko* usually wear precarious *okobo* (a tall version of the *geta*/*zori* sandals) with red straps, whereas *geiko* wear much shorter plain white *zori* sandals. There are other differences in hair and makeup, but those are the quick, obvious ways to tell the difference between a *maiko* and a *geiko* based on their clothes alone. Unfortunately, a lot of *maiko* leave the profession after training instead of becoming full *geiko*, often times to marry, as marriage is prohibited in the *geisha* profession. For this reason, it is increasingly hard to spot *geisha* walking around. As of 2020, there were only a total of around 300 *geiko* and *maiko* combined in Kyoto. Just 80 years ago, there were over 80,000 *geisha* in Kyoto.

tracksuit as he navigated a tiny white dog down the cobbled path between picturesque tiled-roofed shops.

Our guide froze as we were about to cross the street in the man's direction. He looked left and right and then promptly hopped to the pavement underneath an overhang to the left of the intersection. He gestured Amey and I over, and we followed after giving each other a confused look.

"That guy over there is the local *yakuza* boss," he said in a whisper.

"What?" I asked, taking another look at the elderly man in his track shoes with the fluffy dog, which was probably a Shih Tzu or Maltese. It was hard to tell from the distance as he ambled along.

"Yes, and we really don't want to attract his notice."

We gave him another speculative look.

"How do you know it's him?" I asked.

The man was still relatively distant, and I couldn't decipher any of his features. The guide elaborated.

"Do you see those men on the corner in front of where he's approaching? The ones standing in front of the shop doors?"

I nodded. "Yes, what about them?"

"Those are his bodyguards," he said. "Look at how they are standing. Look at the dark sunglasses."

Now that he had drawn attention to it, I saw what he meant. They looked almost like dolls, they were so still. And the fact that they were both standing in such a position as to keep an eye on the old man, both wearing identical sunglasses, and both seeming to have an alert tension to them that rebutted any argument that they just happened to be a couple of guys standing in front of shop doors, jeans and casual coats notwithstanding.

"There are most assuredly additional guards behind him. He might look like he's alone, but he is not."

"How did you figure this out?" I asked again. He had clearly been primed with what to watch for.

"You live here long enough, and you learn," he said. "I have met him a couple of times, but I try to stay clear. As it is, we're across the street from his men, and I don't want to stay here any longer. Let's head that way," he said pointing down the street, away from the intersection that the group of *yakuza* was approaching. We proceeded on with our tour, just a little more tense than we had been before.

I wasn't brave enough to try to get a photo of the gangster. 2008 wasn't 2023. No one walked around glued to their cell phone, and most people still used separate cameras to take high quality photos, including me. It would have been very conspicuous, and after what Professor Wilson had told me at the beginning of the semester, I was happy to let my *yakuza* sighting be only a memory. There may not have been pics, but the scene is frozen in my mind, sharp as a knife, ridiculous in its prosaicness and yet mildly terrifying.[5]

---

[5] In writing this essay, I looked up the name of the local Kyoto *yakuza* and learned that in 2005, shortly before our visit, the Seventh *Aizukotetsu-kai*, which is probably the largest *yakuza* organization in Kyoto, formed an alliance with the Sixth *Yamaguchi-gumi* (the largest *yakuza* group in the country). As of 2021, there are only approximately 50 members in the Seventh *Aizukotetsu-kai*, according to the Japanese National Policy Agency, which tracks such things. I can't imagine the man I saw fifteen years ago is still the head of the *Aizukotetsu-kai* now, as he was definitely in his eighties back then. Both he and his fluffy, white dog are just dust and memories now.

AINOTE

I made this ink and watercolor sketch from a photograph I took of the crowded Kiyomizu-dera (Pure Water) Temple. I was standing at an overlook in Kyoto, Japan during Golden Week, in May, 2008. For just ¥400 ($4.00), you can get an amazing view of Kyoto.

An old, rusted truck,
vines entwine the chassis—solid
frozen forever.

Bristling goosebumps,
marching along my forearm,
remind me again.

Water clings to boots.
The damp seeps through my façade—
refreshing tears fall.

The night is silent
but for the hum and rustle.
Unease settles in.

A piece of my flesh
will always belong to him,
unmet need lingers.

Sun glints on silver—
blue eyes pierce my soul, hands touch,
curling together.

Soft words from pretty mouths
kiss my skin like butterflies.
Here—gone tomorrow.

I WAS A DAY-OLD CHRISTMAS CAKE

I celebrated my 31st birthday while living in Japan. I came to law as a second career and was already in my late 20s by the time I got my act together, finished college, and applied and was accepted. It was not unusual to be an older student in law school. We had some students in my class at University of Florida already in their 40s or older. We also had students in my class who were 19 when they started law school, and, in some respects, they were much less equipped for the type of education law school provides than us old fogies. However, the average student was in their early 20s, most coming directly from undergrad. In the end, no matter our individual ages, we all learned in a trial by fire. I just happened to come to the firing squad later than most.

My circuitous educational journey notwithstanding, I never felt older in law school than I did when I lived in Japan. It was a combination of the gender expectations strictly applied to Japanese women (even as late as 2008) along with the fact the Japanese have a defined term for any unmarried woman over the age of 25. I was a day-old Christmas cake, or more literally a "leftover or unsold *kurisumasu keki.*" If you're wondering why that's such an insulting thing, think about it like this:

"No one wants a Christmas cake after the 25th, and no one wants a woman older than 25."

Looking back, it seems preposterous. I'm 46 now, and I can't even imagine thinking my life would end at 25 if I didn't find a husband. I didn't even marry for the first time until I was 35. But to further highlight how serious this issue is for the Japanese, here are some facts. In 2008, Japanese women only earned approximately 47% as much as Japanese men. They were expected to quit their jobs when they married and become the household manager. As a woman, if you didn't quit your job, it would bring shame on your husband and family. Were you working because you didn't think your husband could provide? Did you not take your role in the family seriously? Were you not willing to prioritize appropriately? These were just some of the questions that might be going through the minds of others if a Japanese woman continued to work after marriage in Japan.

As far as I recall, at that time, there were only two women in the Japanese Diet (essentially the legislative branch of the Japanese government, like our Congress). Neither of these ladies were married, and one of them was the daughter of a Diet member. The Diet in Japan has a lot of legacy participation inside families, which explains why one was a daughter. She was perhaps the only child. My female classmates reported to me that there were no female *bengoshi* (trial attorneys) at any of the functions they attended.[1] A

---

[1] The story of how *bengoshi* are made is one that is incredibly interesting. I posit that the lack of female *bengoshi* certainly has something to do with Japan's culture of quitting once you are married, but this concept is exponentially compounded by the fact that becoming a licensed attorney in Japan used to be considerably harder than in the United States or anywhere in the western world. When I was living there, the average student studied for seven years before passing the Japanese bar exam. Often these men would take

couple of our classmates in the program were Japanese nationals who were either attending law school in the United States or studying at Temple University Japan in pursuit of an LL.M (masters in law).

One of them was only back in Japan from Tulsa for the semester. She was in her thirties as well, so she was well past the average age for a law student. We had a long conversation with her about her situation, and she made it clear to us that her choices were—quit and get married or work and forego a family. There was no third option if she wanted to live in Japan in the year 2008. Not 1950! Not 1970! 2008. It was depressing just to hear about it from her, but the micro-aggressions of living in Tokyo as a woman (foreign or otherwise) were constant needles picking at my soul a millimeter at a time.

Often, my male colleagues were approached by men, chatted up, invited random places, and treated like celebrities on the train. My female colleagues and I were never talked to. Ever. I didn't even realize that this was a common practice towards the guys in our

---

baito (part time jobs) and live subsistence lives where they did nothing but work low-paying jobs and study for the exam until they passed it. The passage rate historically was approximately 2% per year. The Japanese realized this was a problem, and by the time I was living there, they had begun to create specific programs to study law, like western law schools, and were attempting to increase the bar passage rates. Because the smartest Japanese people tend to start in the public sector rather than the private sector, and the highest paid public-sector jobs were *bengoshi*, the brightest minds in Japan would spend years wasted in a kind of stasis where they worked menial labor just to continue studying with the hopes of beginning their careers as lawyers. This is a monumental waste of critically important human capital. I have not dug deeply into how things have changed over the last seventeen years, but I find the entire issue exceedingly interesting.

group until Carrie and I just happened to be present when a group of Japanese men came up to us at the train station and started chatting up the guys in our class. Only the guys. They wanted to know why the guys were here, and upon learning they would be American lawyers, wanted to exchange numbers and stay in touch for business purposes. This was on a train platform. If you're not aware, the Japanese are almost never willing to approach a stranger in public that they don't already know for purely social reasons without a formal introduction. I say almost never, because I'm pretty sure the answer is never, but I was present for one of the exceptions.

In stark contrast, the same friend and I were once approached on a train platform by a lone Japanese woman who asked us in English where we were from. She was small and a little square with shortish, nondescript dark hair, glasses, and plain features. She wore a skirt and blazer and basically blended into the background of Tokyo. If she hadn't spoken to me, I never would have noticed her or remembered if I ever saw her again. But our conversation etches her in my mind forever, a physical rendering of the despair felt by any Japanese woman who had briefly escaped the cage. Only briefly.

"America," Carrie said, and I nodded.

The woman whose name I don't know and couldn't even remember if she ever told it to us began to speak.

"I lived in America for five years," she said. Her face was a mixture of exhilaration and longing at the memories flickering behind her eyes.

"Did you study there?" I asked.

"My company sent me to learn there," she said, "because I knew English." This was a common practice among larger Japanese companies. Companies would send employees to either attend American educational institutions as graduate students, shadow American operations or partners, or even just to get jobs at American companies to learn how they do business. At the time, it was unusual to send women, as far as I knew, but a good working grasp of English trumps gender when there's an economic benefit to be had.

"I love America," she said, emotion creeping into her voice. "I was so free. I am not free here. I want to leave and go back. But I can't."

I wanted to cry; to give this woman a hug. The agony of realizing that she was admitting these feelings to total strangers on the train platform because there was literally no one else in her life that she felt she could have this conversation with shredded me. She was a leftover Christmas cake for sure, and she was obviously a working woman, and all she saw when she looked down the path of her life was a desolate wasteland. It was awkward, intense, and heartbreaking. After she bowed and thanked us for our time and got on her train, Carrie and I were silent for a bit. This was a part of Japan that I knew about, that I experienced even as a *gaijin*, but a part that I would never have to accept into my identity the way that poor, forlorn woman already had done. Yes, I too was a day-old Christmas cake, but I could leave that horrific label behind when I left Tokyo and resume my life in America where I was by no means treated with absolute equality, but where my life would be looked at by millions of Japanese women as a panacea.

I don't recount this story to somehow glorify the United States. It's where I was born, where I grew up, where I call home, and where I feel most comfortable, despite our current state of political and social turmoil that finds people's individual rights being continuously abrogated even as gun violence runs rampant and seven-year-old children die on Independence Day because assholes bring guns to the beach and argue over jet skis. If that seems oddly specific, that's because it happened this week in Tampa, Florida, where I live, and I still feel sick knowing that permitless carry went into effect July 1 and a child died three days later, hit by a stray bullet while hiding in a truck as his grandfather physically shielded him from a gun fight. The bullet went through the grandfather's finger and struck the child in the head.

Non sequitur aside, I tell this story because there is a devastating sadness to think that this woman was so unhappy that she'd rather risk the daily discomfort of living in another country on a fourteen-hour time difference from her family than to remain where she was, in the culture that she grew up in and understood intimately. The often violent, xenophobic, homophobic, transphobic, racist, and ruthless America was preferable to the relative safety, both physically and emotionally, of living in Japan. It's a sobering thought, both because as a country the United States should be doing a hell of a lot better than we are—really, no excuses, folks; and because even when we aren't, there are still people that would choose this in a heartbeat over their existing situations, and some of those people live in the largest city in the world with highly advanced technology and some of the longest lifespans.

Despite all these challenges for Japanese women, as a *gaijin*, it seemed as if Japanese men had as much trouble pinpointing my age as I did theirs. Generally, men might not have wanted to talk to me, but they were fine with staring at me in public, particularly on the train, and groping me if the opportunity presented itself. On any given train ride, I would lift my gaze from my phone or a book to invariably catch five pairs of eyes shifting from me to a random part of the car. Unless the man was old. If he was old, he'd just stare right into my face or right into my chest if he was particularly brazen. I guess having zero fucks to give as you age is a universal condition.

One night in Shibuya, I was either forced (or had the opportunity depending on how you choose to frame it) to directly challenge these diametrically opposed realities. It was not long before my 31st birthday, and my friend Amey was still visiting me from Florida. Amey and I met in college in 1997 when we were both randomly assigned to the same suite at an off-campus student apartment complex. She also happened to know my boyfriend at the time, since they both played in a Vampire LARP group. Amey was a goth, and I was a nerd, but we bonded over the fact that we were both incredibly smart, both liked anime, and both got into playing Dungeons and Dragons. Dungeons and Dragons solidly overlaps both goths and nerds. By the time she visited me in Tokyo, we'd been friends for over ten years. The goth and nerd personas had largely been shed, but the love of Japanese food, anime, j-pop, shopping, and Japanese dramas continued as shared interests. When we get together now, we still go shopping and spend time catching up on our respective lives, but we've largely moved on as Japanophiles, except for maybe the food.

At the time, Amey was so excited to visit Japan that she came for three weeks and took an unpaid week off work so she could stay longer than her paid vacation allowance. She was with me over my spring break, and we took that week to travel to Kyoto.[2] Amey and I used to like to go dancing back in the day, so one of the must-do activities was hitting up a club in Shibuya. I can't remember which club we went to, whether Amey found the place or I did, but it was a sprawling club with a bunch of different rooms, some of which

---

[2] See "Yakuza-a-Go-Go" to read more tidbits about Kyoto.

had seating, some of which had dance floors. There was a DJ spinning, and he had caught Amey's full attention, so we spent a good amount of time milling around watching him. At some point, I remember I snagged a table in one of the main areas, and I was sitting there when a handsome, young Japanese guy slid into the chair next to me.

He introduced himself in passable English and asked if I had a boyfriend.

"Yes," I said, giving him an apologetic smile.

"Well, I can be your Japanese boyfriend," he responded, unphased by my admission that I was seeing someone already.

"But I have a boyfriend," I repeated.

"That's OK," he said. "I will be your *Japanese* boyfriend. You can take me to America." The implication was that whoever my partner was, they were not here in Japan with me, so Mr. Young Guy was perfectly willing to be a stand-in. This kid could not have been older than twenty-one. I asked him what he did, and he said he studied accounting.

"How old do you think I am?" I asked. I felt almost bad setting him up this way. Almost.

"Twenty-two?" He said, looking surprised and vaguely alarmed that I had posited the question at all.

The fact that I had asked him to guess my age had put him on the spot in an unexpected way. I was a *gaijin*, however, so the rules of propriety did not apply to me. I gestured up with my left hand, signaling him to go higher.

"Twenty-three?" He tried again.

I shook my head, giving him a small smile. His throat bobbed as he swallowed hard, perhaps sensing the trap.

"Twenty-five?"

I shook my head. In response, he pointed up gingerly, and I nodded. By this time, the discomfort was palpable.

"Twenty-seven?" He asked.

He wasn't green around the gills, but the discomfort had intensified to concern. Again, I shook my head and gestured higher. At this point, I could see that he was steeling himself that he might be hitching his wagon to an old mare. He started to guess again, but I spared him the pain.

"I'm thirty," I said, "almost thirty-one."

I held up three fingers to hit home my point. The young man's attempt to reconcile this completely unsatisfactory number with his desire to find a sugar mamma to take him to America painted his face a picture of blunt calculus, and I had to restrain from laughing.

"It's OK," he said finally, mustering a bright but tense smile. "I can be your Japanese boyfriend."

In his mind, pragmatism won! But, really, is it pragmatic to try to get an older woman who is already seeing someone to take you away to America? As you may suspect, I ultimately declined his generous offer to suffer my decrepit company.

My partner at the time did not find this exchange amusing. My seeming attractiveness to men, whether Japanese or even just the guys in my law program who were routinely seven or more years younger than me, was a constant source of tension during our relationship while I was abroad. I was constantly having to defend my decisions, and the thought of dealing with yet another person asserting control over my behavior was exhausting.[3]

---

[3] See "No Time for Love, Doctor Jones!" for more about my romantic issues during this time.

Living in Tokyo, the entire balancing act of gender and role expectations was an ironic place to be, since I was there to learn and enjoy immersing myself in another culture, not to sew my oats. Additionally, I had researched and applied for this program before I even began dating my partner at that time, so if anything, I had committed to having an experience in Japan before I ever met them. Looking back, the fact that I felt I had to meet these conflicting expectations of being a dutiful girlfriend to an American I had only been dating less than six months, a friend to the guys in my class, a novelty to the Japanese men, and eye candy for all of them was completely ridiculous. I guess fifteen years later, I no longer subscribe to my body and my mind being the purview of anyone else, whether I'm romantically attached to them or otherwise. Romantic attachments require a completely different litmus test now than they did in 2008. It's hard to argue that a man will make my life better when, after 46 years of life, they consistently have not. I'm not an angry man-hating woman bitter about her past relationships. Every person I've loved or believed at the time that I loved taught me something valuable about myself.

Despite this assertion, I'm also not a pessimist about love or future relationships. I never made relationships my goal going into them, but I think it's just as important to not "fall" into a relationship or default to one because someone else wants it. I need to become very intentional in my abstaining from a relationship where one doesn't make sense to me. Finally, I'm an optimist about me and my ability to be happy outside of a relationship. No one person, no societal expectation, and no gender expectation can disabuse me of the notion that, for me, I am enough. I always think I knew this but knowing it and acting on it are different. As I quickly round up to an age double the expiration date in Japan, this knowledge is really freeing because every day is Christmas! I never expire.

AINOTE

I made this ink and watercolor sketch from a photograph I took of Fuji-yama (Mt. Fuji) from the window of a Shinkansen slowing to a stop near Hakone, Japan in May 2008

Energy crackles—
thoughts buzzing through synapses;
mind on the highway.

Fingers move and words
flow out in melodic taps—
poetry becomes.

Wandering the fields,
me, my only company—
I'm never lonely.

Each lash of the whip,
a story unto its own—
arcing through the night.

A beetle swimming
in my pool spurs a rescue—
and lives to shine on.

Clatter of color—
rocks tumble and glitter, shine—
like dice on the board.

NO SOUP FOR YOU!

If you have ever wondered what happens when you truly piss off a Japanese waiter, it is both wildly anticlimactic and simultaneously very humiliating, because you won't feel that super sick burn for a good twenty minutes after it's done, but when you do, you just have to slink away knowing everyone else caught on before you. Before we get to that, let me say that as a group of well-meaning but ultimately *baka gaijin*, my TUJ class had their fair share of unfortunate incidents with waitstaff at restaurants. One such minor incident occurred when my friend Jennifer, myself, and my partner visiting me in Tokyo went out for *okonomiyaki* (literally translated to anything you want grilled or grilled as you like it). My partner had been really wanting to try *okonomiyaki*, so we made an evening of it and went to a small restaurant in Shinjuku, and Jennifer came along, also eager to experience the cuisine.

If you are unfamiliar with it, *okonomiyaki* is often described as a Japanese savory pancake. I find this description to be wildly inaccurate for the purpose of actually understanding what you are eating when you eat *okinomiyaki*. In my opinion, the actual literal translation is more accurate as to what you're getting when you sit down for *okonomiyaki*. The word directly translates to "fried on a griddle", and the reality of the dish is that it basically is anything you want, placed in a pile, griddled with a small amount of batter, and then consumed with sauces. When you eat *okonomiyaki*, it's much more about the cabbage and proteins than it is the batter. The batter is essentially the bare minimum needed to bind all the rest of the ingredients together. It's like calling a piece of chicken that's dipped in flour and egg and then fried a piece of French toast. Yes, there's eggs and flour in French toast, but it sure as hell isn't the same as fried chicken. Maybe that's just my lawyerly need for precision, but there you have it.

Originating in Osaka, *okonomiyaki* is a *teppan* (a griddle — you might be familiar with the word *teppanyaki* which literally means "grill fired") style meal served on a hot metal grill in the center of the table. Each person selects their ingredients, which almost always starts with a liberal base of cabbage and adds meat or seafood and various seasonings into the batter, including *dashi* (fish flakes, commonly used as the base for soup broths, such as miso soup). The waiter will bring the ingredients and then you will dump them out in a pile onto your griddle and grill them up into a "pancake" and top it with things like Japanese mayo, *okonomiyaki* sauce (a very savory sauce similar to Worcestershire sauce or *tonkatsu* sauce), *aonori* (seaweed flakes), *katsuboshi* (bonito flakes— dried and flaked tuna), and pickled ginger. These are also pretty common toppings for Japanese street foods, such as *takoyaki* (fried octopus balls). You can also get *okanomiyaki* Kyoto style from a street vendor, and it's folded almost like a taco. This version of *okonomiyaki* is made twenty at a time on a large grill with not nearly as much customization as Osaka style. It starts with a layer of batter on the griddle, then piles of cabbage, surimi, bean sprouts, tiny, dried shrimps, whatever other toppings, and finally a whole egg cracked into the center. Then it's folded in half and covered in mayo and eaten. I actually prefer my *okinomiyaki* Kyoto style, although my sister still cringes when she remembers me taunting her with the little dried shrimp liberally dotted throughout, which still had their shells and eyeballs.

That night in Shinjuku, Jennifer, my partner, and I were seated at a half booth for four with a griddle set into the middle of the table large enough to accommodate an individual cooking surface for each anticipated diner. The ambience was that of a good steak house in the United States—relatively quiet, secluded, and private, with low ambient lighting and dark décor. After being seated, we did the usual thing and asked our server for an *Eigo no menu* (English menu). It was not often that restaurants printed an English menu, but it was more common in establishments where you couldn't really rely on a photograph of the food to understand what it was you were ordering, which was definitely the case for *okonomiyaki*. We made our request, and the server seemed to hesitate for a moment before moving away to locate the menus.

Jennifer took that opportunity to mutter something sarcastic in English. I can't remember precisely what she said, but it was something like "Couldn't he tell we were speaking English and would want English menus?" She wasn't trying to be rude. I think she was just making a joke. We had all suffered the frustration of trying to communicate in Tokyo. Yes, I know. We were the *gaijin*. Americans often make a big stink about how if you're going to visit America, you should speak English. But we sometimes still expect everyone else on this giant planet to speak the one language we happen to have learned growing up and to accommodate our needs for English materials automatically. The privilege of the fact that the circumstance of our birth means that our assigned language is the one most spoken around the entire world is quite literally lost on most English-speaking people.

When the waiter returned with the English menus, he bent his head low and spoke directly to Jennifer.

"I am studying English in university," he said in English. "You should be careful what you say, because you don't really know, do you?" Jennifer's eyes widened and she turned pink in embarrassment.

"You're right," she muttered softly and made a weak apology. The offense to the server in this case was mild. After he made his point, he might have been a little formal and cold compared to the usual server, but he continued to do his job, and we tried not to be assholes any more than we already had by that point. In this case, the lesson was this. Don't assume people should know your language, but also don't assume they don't know it! I don't want to paint Jennifer as a jerk, since she most certainly was not one. This was a lesson we all learned that day, not just her, and it was one we took with us on many future dining experiences together.

I particularly remember Jennifer and a couple of us at a restaurant one night, and I was really missing American food and particularly TexMex. I made either the mistake or the incredibly amazing decision, however you decide to view it, of ordering a "Mexican pizza" for dinner. It was something Jennifer and I had decided to share, so maybe it was both our dubious decisions. This was another instance where there was an English menu, although perhaps a picture menu would have given us a better idea of what to expect from a "Mexican pizza." When our food arrived, smack in the middle was a completely raw egg, floating around jovially on the fully cooked pizza. I honestly can't recall what other toppings were even on this monstrosity (Or was it a work of art? You decide!) that might have qualified it as Mexican, but you know what? No one was accosted or insulted. No faces were made—well, maybe some carefully hidden faces. No angry demands made to take it away. We just had a laugh, sucked it up, and figured out how to eat the thing. In case you're interested, a knife and fork seemed to be the least messy way to go. Chopsticks were not going to cut it for that one.

All this brings me to the night where we really and truly offended our waitstaff, and it was a sad night indeed. There was a restaurant right near our school that we all absolutely loved to frequent. The bottom floor was set up with a conveyor belt. One of my favorite conveyor belt sushi restaurants was in Ueno, and it was a cramped space with two chefs in the middle and a tiny belt that circled them with a bar of stools in front of it. This place, however, sprawled. There were tables and booths all along a massive kitchen area, and the long conveyor belt wound through the whole bottom floor of the restaurant, carrying little plates of nigiri, sashimi, salads, octopus, and more past every booth and table in the place. We would go there often, and my favorite sushi was a type of nigiri that I've only seen two places outside of Japan. One being in Hawaii at a conveyor belt sushi restaurant on the Big Island, and the other in Orlando, Florida at EDOBoy, a standing sushi restaurant that is fantastic. EDOBoy actually "torches" what they call their *sake-kewpie*, which means they assemble the nigiri and then run a small butane torch over it, and it is yum yum yum yum. It's not the same at EDOBoy as is in Tokyo, but it is still great. Also, they have the best miso soup I've ever had outside of Japan, so if you're ever visiting Orlando, make your way to the Colonialtown North area and book at EDOBoy. You will not regret it. Also, if you invite me, I will for sure drive over from Tampa to join you.

Anyway, this nigiri sushi as originally designed starts with the usual mound of rice, then with a slice of fresh, raw salmon on top, a light squiggle of Japanese mayo, and finally a tiny sprinkle of super-fine mandoline-sliced onions. This simple piece of food is 100% the way to my heart, and when I go back to Japan, I plan to locate a place that sells this salmon nigiri every single day that I am there and gorge myself. Hopefully, that will hold me over for the next fifteen years. So now that you understand how very much I love this particular nigiri, I can get to the point.

That night, instead of grabbing a couple of tables at the bottom floor, we decided to head upstairs where the restaurant had its larger tables. There were probably eight or ten of us, and the tables upstairs could accommodate that size party. Unlike the bottom floor, there was no conveyor belt whisking the ambrosia of the gods around to each table, so we had to rely on humans to bring us our food. I and my friend Becca were both really in the mood for the salmon nigiri, so Becca flagged down our waiter and asked for "four orders of *sake* salmon." Now, *sake* means salmon in Japanese. So, Becca asked for salmon salmon. Also, our placement of the order failed to specify that we were asking for nigiri. It probably just sounded like gibberish to the waiter. If this was the United States, the server probably would have stopped and asked us again what we wanted and confirmed it by showing us the menu, but I suspect in this case it was a mix of not wanting to insult us by highlighting the fact we were completely unintelligible and not wanting to appear incompetent. Whatever the impetus, the waiter took that order and left.

It was about fifteen minutes later when the waiter brought around four orders of yakisoba.[1] "Sake salmon" to "yakisoba". It was a reasonable enough translation, but it was not what we ordered. In the United States, the custom is just to explain that this was not what was ordered and send it back for the correct dish. The

---

[1] If you are unfamiliar, yakisoba is a type of wheat noodle that looks a bit like ramen, perhaps a bit thicker but not thick like udon, and it is usually served stir fried with soy, meat, and vegetables similarly to lo mein in Chinese food.

customer is always right, after all. In Japan, that was apparently something you just do not do. You do not send food back under any circumstance. By the time we realized this, however, the damage was done. Becca had politely told the waitstaff that this was not what she ordered and asked them to take it back, and they did. They took it back, certainly, but then they never came back to our table again. That was it. We were persona non grata from that moment forward. Our friend Mae, a Japanese-born student at an American law school and part of our class, was there with us, and she was so horrifically embarrassed by what we'd done that the moment the waiters left with the food, she sprang up and fled. She didn't even stick around to give us an explanation of our massive misstep, just said that she was too ashamed to be with us and left. Poof! She was gone.

The rest of us just sat around in a state of intense discomfort. We didn't know what to do. We wanted to apologize and explain, but we could not get a single waiter to come back to the table. They just pretended like the large group of *gaijin* in the middle of the room did not exist. After trying to figure out what to do for another twenty minutes or so, we finally just up and left. You may be wondering: *How does a server just leave a table and not come back? That doesn't seem possible logistically.* The answer is that we already had our check. In Japan, the custom in almost every restaurant (except maybe the most fancy of places) is that after every interaction with a server, they will bring by a paper check and leave it at the table. There's usually a little cup set up on the table where the check lives. You're allowed to be at the restaurant as long as you want, and you can order as much as you want. If you place another order, the server will take your current check and bring back your new order and an updated check, so you always have the most current check at your table. Whenever you are ready to depart, you just take that paper slip to the cashier who is at the entrance to the restaurant, and you pay there. Tipping is not only not expected in Japan but will usually be rebuffed, and in some cases seen as insulting, so no tips are left at the table or paid when you cash out your check.

What this meant for us at the time was that we basically had to sit there shamed and ignored until we had given up catching anyone's attention to apologize, take the check sitting in the cup on our table that includes the four orders of yakisoba that we rudely sent back, and pay the entire bill before leaving the restaurant. It was mortifying. I could see why Mae had bailed on us instantly. There was no way to come back from it. The shame was already upon us. If you think I'm recounting this story because I fault the waiters, I don't. If you think I'm recounting it to shame my friend who placed the order in the first place and sent the food back, I'm not. It was just one of those incidents where two cultures are just completely diametrically opposite regarding what is considered the usual course of action, and we were not prepared. What we considered an innocent mistake easily rectified, they considered a massive breach of social contract. It was a humbling lesson on Japanese etiquette but also no one's fault. Perhaps we should have known. Realistically, however, every culture on this tiny blue rock of ours has a million and one rules that its citizens internalize osmotically, and it's nearly impossible to correctly guess all the time. This was that one, crucial, time when we dropped the ball in a big way. So, I look back now, and I'm amazed and slightly amused that we managed to thoroughly piss off a group of waiters so much that they silent-treatmented us all the way out of the restaurant, but it definitely impacted our friend Mae, who we did apologize to when we saw her next. I never did go back to that top portion of restaurant, although I can't speak for any of the others, but I did still run in to grab sushi from the conveyor belt below. I mercifully didn't have to rely on waitstaff to lift their ban for that.

AINOTE

I made this ink and watercolor sketch from a photograph of the sculpture "The Weeper" by artists and married couple, François-Xavier Lalanne and Claude Lalanne. Permanent exhibit of the Hakone Open Air Museum in Hakone, Japan. Photo was taken in May 2008.

Slipping softly to
soundless slumber—drifting down,
slowly, into dark.

Exhaustion breaks like
dawn against my blinking eyes—
bleary in the night.

Submerging slowly,
thoughts quiescent in the night.
So when will I sleep?

Cold air blows on me;
dog paws twitch in the darkness.
Still, sleep does not come.

Tilting at windmills—
I don't know why I miss you,
but it maddens me.

Under a thin sheet,
I turn away from your ghost—
alone in my bed.

MIND THE GAP

The Japanese people are known around the world as some of the nicest people with which to interact. Visitors to Japan often laud the politeness and congeniality of every single Japanese person they meet. While the surface of each such interaction is polite, the deeper feelings can often be very different from those expressed. This is something I learned both from my Japanese Law professor and from just spending months in the country.

The Japanese even have special words for their feelings, which are collectively called *honne-tatemae*. *Honne* means "spoken truth" and *tatamae* means "façade". Professor Wilson used to translate this roughly as skin and bone. What you see isn't what the person is feeling deeply. Many cultures have the idea that your public behavior and private feelings are separate, but the Japanese take this concept to the absolute extreme. It is exceedingly rare to be exposed to the true feelings even of people you know well. With a stranger, you can generally just forget it!

And yet, that's just what happened while jean shopping at the Gap in Harajuku one sunny day near the end of my semester. The Gap was a massive three-story superstore of American brand clothing. The store in Harajuku closed permanently a year after I left in Tokyo. I don't know if it was due to customer-service related issues, but perhaps my experience wasn't as unique as it seemed.

Whatever the result, I still found the experience shocking at the time.

I loved the Ometesando area inside Harajuku, and I would wander there frequently during the day before classes and eat crepes from street vendors, browse shops, and play tourist at the local shrines. The crepe vendors were particularly amazing. They would roll the delicate pancakes into a cone shape and fill them with cheesecake or ice cream and chocolate sauce. I remember scandalizing one of the crepe stands by once asking for both a slice of cheesecake and a scoop of ice cream in a single crepe. I'm pretty sure that was an epic faux pas, but they made it anyway, because... *tatemae*. They somehow didn't charge me double, which also led me to believe that literally no one would order off-menu like that except a *baka gaijin* (stupid foreigner). That day, I was happy to be that stupid foreigner. Best crepe I've ever had![1]

---

[1] Although the Japanese have a specific concept for it, they are not the only ones who put on a public face in society, and I certainly did my share of relying on a façade when in polite company in Japan. On one particular instance, my friend Becky and I decided to visit a tea shop that specialized in tools for tea ceremony. Becky was very interested in tea ceremony and *matcha* (green tea leaves ground into powder and suspended in water instead of steeped). I was not. Don't get me wrong. I enjoyed the cultural aspects of tea ceremony, but not so much imbibing the *matcha*. I'm a supertaster and drinking *matcha* for me is like getting tackled on a grassy field and having my face ground into the dirt and grass and then be expected to chew it. I've had wheatgrass before as well which is strong, but *matcha* is like if someone took wheatgrass and amplified it by ten times and then asked me to sip it slowly and savor it. It's absolutely dreadful, and I've had to drink it a couple of times to maintain my status as a civilized *gaijin*. The evening in question, the tea shop was about to close when we arrived, and we started to make our apologies and say we would come back another time, but the little old man

who ran the shop beamed at us and asked us if we'd ever had real *matcha* before.

"No," said Becky with enthusiasm. "I really want to try it. I love *matcha* in the United States."

I adore Becky, but I damned her to hell in that instant! She had just issued a social challenge to the shopkeeper. To this day, I don't know if he was expressing his *honne* or *tatamae* when he invited us upstairs to the study area to make us "real" matcha when he should have been readying to end his day. He certainly looked sincere, but that's the point of this. It always seems sincere unless you're very clued into the minutiae, which we definitely were not. So, for all I know it could have been an elaborate dance of *tatamae* that we could have just avoided if we'd said something like "Oh, we don't want to inconvenience you, sir" and bowing as we insisted that we go back to the door. Instead, we essentially stumbled into asking for an invitation because we didn't know better.

With big smiles, genuine for Becky, and hopefully fake enough for me, we followed him up the stairs to a room above the shop. He guided us to a few stuffed chairs around a small table and began to bring over a selection of implements, including a pot of acid-green powder, a small metal sieve, a tiny wooden scoop (*chashaku*), a bamboo whisk (*chasen*), two bowls (*chawan*) and a pot of water. He explained to us the importance of each tool and how they would be used in formal tea ceremony, but he said he was just going to make some straightforward *matcha* for us. Because *matcha* isn't designed to get its flavor or texture from steeping, steeping the tea is not as important as the whisking. In total fairness, the process for making *matcha* tea and the reasons for tea ceremony itself, including the time it takes to engage, the special room used by participants, the measuring, the whisking, the shape of the bowl it's drunk from, was all very interesting. However, it was hard to relax and enjoy the interesting aspects knowing that I was going to have to pretend to relish the pond scum I would be forced to taste at the end. Traditional *matcha* tea isn't made to be steeped, so boiling water isn't used. It's just hot water, and you can usually drink it pretty quickly, which makes sense, since you want your tea powder to stay suspended. One shouldn't wait to drink it and risk the suspension separating. He made the common form of *matcha* called *usucha* (thin) matcha for us. *Usucha* is thinner, which means it's easier to

Another aspect of Japan (at least in 2008 while they were still suffering from decades of stagflation) is that they tended to grossly overstaff jobs. My local Starbucks in Temple Terrace, Florida usually has anywhere between one and two employees working the register and the machines during slow times and maybe three or four during exceptionally busy times. In Tokyo, a Starbucks might

---

drink, but it also foams up a bunch, which is a texture I also do not enjoy. He continued to beam at us as he carefully handed us each a bowl and urged us to drink. I looked into my bowl of bright green foam and tried to keep my face smooth. Becky went first and sipped enthusiastically.

"It's so delicious," she said with genuine delight.

I smiled and hoped the smile looked not like the rigid death mask it really felt like from the inside and took a tentative sip, trying not to get foam all over my face. It tasted even worse than I'd imagined, and it took every ounce of my being to take a substantial sip and swallow it down without choking. How much of this would I have to drink to be polite? I absolutely could not finish the whole bowl. Given my propensity for public embarrassment, you may think that I lost it and spit it all over the nice old gentleman, but you'd be wrong. I just bore it. I just sipped it and sipped it, and nodded and smiled and said, "this is all so interesting" since I wasn't a great liar. I managed to eventually get most of the actual liquid out, leaving a pile of foam in the bowl. I suspected he wouldn't be as offended if it was just foam leftover, but luckily for me, Becky had completely polished hers off and was bright-eyed and so very enthusiastic. She ended up buying some simple tools to make her own *matcha* at home, and thank all the Shinto gods, because I would not have been able to take it that far. My goal that evening was just to leave that shopkeeper thinking that he'd met some nice, polite *gaijin* who were interested in tea ceremony and Japanese culture, and that he hadn't wasted a half hour showing us all a portion of Japanese tradition that was critically important to how the Japanese interacted with each other historically.

"That was so much fun," Becky said as we left.

"It really was," I agreed. I kept to myself my worry that all I would taste whenever I ate or drank anything for the next week was a football field.

have two separate people at each register, one to take the order, and the other to prep the cup and hand it off to someone who pumps syrups. A fourth person might work the espresso machine, and then a fifth person adds toppings, and you see what I'm getting at here. Businesses in Japan had so many people servicing the customer that they almost couldn't fit behind the counter.

The Gap was no exception. Perhaps the large number of staff was easy to support since they charged ¥10,000 ($100 USD) for a pair of jeans in 2008. That was probably a 45% markup over what the same jeans would have cost in the States at the time.

What does all of this have to do with *honne-tatemae*? Well, by this point, I had been living in Tokyo for probably four months. The longer I lived there, the more I began to see the nuances of Japanese politeness. It became apparent to me when people were genuinely being nice versus just plastering on the pleasant and mild façade, which was frankly the vast majority of the time. It also becomes harder to ignore the tiny signs when everyone conducts themselves on the limited range of very polite to ultra-polite.

When entering any establishment, even a branded stall in a larger mall department store, I would be welcomed with "*Irasshaimase!*" (Welcome!) But if I wanted to try on a knit sweater while clothes shopping, the girls would politely tell me that it was prohibited by store policy to try on the sweater without purchasing it first because my chest was too big and would stretch the garment. At that time, I was an extra small in most tops. I'm still a small fifteen years later. But they saw a 32DD—a bra size that didn't exist in Japan—and assumed that the knitwear would not survive my gargantuan, anime boobs. This information was always delivered in the politest of ways with a detailed explanation rather than a "no," and there was not a hint of *honne* in the censure of my chest.

In contradiction to the ultra-polite refusal to let me irrevocably disfigure a sweater, the checkout person at that Gap in Harajuku was in exceptionally rare form one afternoon while I was shopping. I, lacking better judgment, was missing home and decided to purchase two pairs of jeans. If you recall, this was in excess of $200 on a student's budget. When I took my jeans to the counter to check out, there were two ladies manning each register. One girl rang up my purchases, while the other one folded and packed my pants neatly into a bag. I believe what happened that day is that the packer somehow got ahead of the cashier.

The register didn't have a digital display facing me, so I didn't realize until I was holding my receipt that I was only charged for one pair of jeans instead of the two I was taking home.

"*Sumimasen*," I said, (Excuse me) after the girl finished her small bow and presented me with the bag.

I gestured to the receipt and tried to explain.

"*Ni jeansu*," (Two pairs of jeans) I said.

Without even looking at what I was pointing at, she raised her arms in a large cross in front of her body, like a football referee, and yelled "No Discount!" in English.

At this point, I was taken aback. It was almost as shocking as the time that guy on the train to Odaiba pretended to stumble into me, groped me hard with a palm to my vagina, and then stumbled off the train before I could confront him. Actually, let's be real. It was more shocking, since I had come to expect old men to pretend to be drunk and to fully palm my lady bits as they knock into me and then flee the train car while I yelled after them, "Hey, you just groped me!" as everyone on the train car looked on in interest. This act has a name in Japan and is called a *chikan* attack. It's so common that approximately 48% off Japanese women have suffered a *chikan* attack.

Not only had this Gap employee yelled at me and caused a public scene, but I was only trying show her that she had failed to charge me for a pair of $100 jeans. If I was less of a do-gooder, I probably would have walked out thinking, *Whatever lady... if you're going to be that way...*

But, instead, I tried again. I leaned over the counter and held my finger up in a two. With my other hand, I slapped the receipt down and said *"Ni jeansu o kaimashita"* (I bought two pairs of jeans).

She finally registered that I was trying to show her something and looked at the receipt.

"Oohhhhh," she said in as she realized the mistake. "*Arigatou gosaimasu*" (Thank you very much). And then the giant arm X disappeared and the bowing commenced.[2] She must have bowed

---

[2] The finger X, hand X, or forearm X (you may have noticed 🙅 among your emojis and wondered about it) is a common sign employed by Japanese people to inform someone else that they either cannot do something they are about to do or be somewhere they are about to go. I was once given a forearm X by a security guard when I attempted to walk through an entrance that was closed off, and sometimes a finger X or hand X, usually held lower on the body, if something I wanted wasn't available in a store or not an option at a restaurant. Usually, it would appear when asking for an *Eigo no menu* (English menu). The gesture will often be used in lieu of saying "No." Sometimes it will accompany the "No", but Japanese people generally, really, absolutely hate to say *iie*, or "no". Maybe that's because the literal translation of *iie* is "That's incorrect." And I can see how it might be rude to tell someone they are being incorrect. In his book <u>Dave Barry Does Japan</u>, the American humor writer David Barry recounts a story of his wife trying to book a plane ticket from one part of Japan to another and going around and around with the

five times as she rang up the second pair of jeans, and I handed back my credit card to be charged a second time.

I left that store having truly seen someone's *honne*—both when she lost it on me and then again when she realized I was just trying to be helpful by not scamming the store out of a pair of jeans. I don't know how stores handle inventory discrepancies in Japan, but I suspect that there could have been actual consequences to being the one on the register when it came up short. Conversely, given how many extra people were involved in the checkout process, I also suspect that being undercharged happens regularly.

I do sometimes wish I could employ the finger, hand, or arm X in my daily life. There is something very satisfying about a physical denial that goes beyond telling another person "no". Perhaps the Japanese also get such satisfaction from even these small gestures. It's like getting to flip someone off or swipe your hand under your chin without it actually being obscene, just assertive. Maybe if I'd thought of it, I could have run after that fake-drunk groper on the train and chased him through the Shibara-fūto station rage-screaming nonsense while making a giant arm X. It might not have been as amusing to him if I took people's attention and focused it on him with signs they would know even if my words were incomprehensible. I mean, the Japanese word for pervert is *hentai*, which many people know from the style of anime that utilizes tentacles or other non-human appendages for penetrative

---

booking agent who would not just come out and say that there were no flights available on that route. Instead, the agent just kept suggesting that the Barrys take the train instead. It was a very frustrating conversation for both Mr. Barry's wife and the Japanese booking agent, since one could not pick up on the subtle fact that these repeated suggestions were the Japanese way of saying "no", and the other could not throw up a finger X on a phone conversation to signal that what the person was asking for was not possible.

acts, usually violent, on cartoon women.[3] I know this word too, but it just didn't seem appropriate for a person just copping a feel. An arm X in the face, though, followed by chasing and deranged ravings, yes! Perhaps he would have thought twice about groping a *baka gaijin*. Stick to the tentacle cartoons, dude!

---

[3] Fun fact, or maybe not fun, actually… but the pornographic anime films known as *hentai* came into existence because the Japanese definition of obscenity under Article 175 of the Criminal Code is highly debated. It's such a gray area and so bizarrely policed that most pornography makers have self-censored their own media by either blurring the area where penetration might be occurring, using elaborately large merkins (pubic wigs) to cover genitals, or depicting completely unrealistic scenes, like tentacles penetrating cartoon women. There has been the odd case of *hentai* being "too realistic" which has resulted in monetary fines and threatened jail sentences for those convicted, even as late as 2013. So, if you've ever wondered about why the Japanese favor tentacles or machines in their porno over actual penises, now you know. Penises are actually reserved for family festivals. Check out my essay "Kanamara Matsuri: The Festival of the Steel Phallus" to learn more.

AINOTE

I made this ink and watercolor sketch from a photograph of a shirt that I found in a "vintage American" menswear shop in Ueno, Tokyo, January 2008

Still not a robot,
I think and feel and write words—
flesh and bone and meat.

Sitting in your mind,
I weigh on you like a ghost—

anchored in the past.
Petals curl and droop,
choked by the glazed heat, air steamed—
withered in the fire.

Cannot think from rage—
Blood working its way through veins.
Stop and break, or cry.

A coyote howls
near my house in the suburbs.
A wild dog haunts.

I SKULL FUCK... AND OTHER ENGRISH ATROCITIES

In the pre-smartphone era of the mid-2000s, one of the primary forms of entertainment for any English-speaking *gaijin* living in Japan was stumbling across egregious instances of "Engrish."[1] Engrish in the wild was very common in a time before the Google Translate app existed and before the near instantaneous spread of

---

[1] "Engrish" is a term that is a catch all for any form of defective English, usually because the words are either inaccurate, grammatically incorrect, or downright nonsensical. Because so much comes from a place of political incorrectness, the word itself is a parody of the average Japanese person's struggle to pronounce the word English. It may be funny to those of us who can pronounce an L, but the simple fact is that Japanese people never learn the letter L. They don't even have that letter in Japanese. They have an R, but Japanese Rs are so slurry as to sound more like something between an R and an L. So if your name is Bill, your name would be pronounced Bi-ru, but the ru would be pronounced with the tongue folded near the back teeth which results in a really slurry R-L sound. It's my personal theory that Sofia Coppola used Bill in Lost in Translation not because the actor was Bill Murray but because the name Bill is rough on the Japanese to pronounce. My own name, which is heavily dependent on Ls sounds pretty hilarious in Japanese. Alia Luria becomes Ah-ri-ah Ru-ri-ah. And you thought it was a tongue twister in English!

communications, e.g., going viral. I can't say for sure how it is now, since I still need to get myself back to Japan for a visit, but back in the day, if you wanted to see a four-year-old boy wearing a t-shirt that said "fuck" on it in 50 different places being dragged along the street by his mother, you either had to live in Asia or specifically look for it online, like on Engrish.com or on 4chan.

Richard Dawkins, in his 1970s book <u>The Selfish Gene</u>, coined the term "memetics" on which we base the commonly used term "meme" and is therefore, in a scholarly sense, or in my opinion anyway, the forefather of all memes. 4chan is an image-based community of forums, a precursor to Reddit, and commonly considered to be the Internet's primary source for early meme generation. In my own selfish way, I prefer to think of the propagation of memes to be credited to Richard Dawkins, because we all know that 4chan was started by a fifteen-year-old high school student and on any given day still reflects its roots pretty strongly.

My own thesis on the origin of the modern meme is that the Japanese people should be credited with the development and early distribution of memes. It was old school. It was analog. It was completely unintentional, which is another hallmark of an excellent meme. And it was fucking hilarious. My case in three arguments:

ONE: 4chan, which started in 2003, basically just ripped off 2chan, a Japanese bulletin board system formally named Futuba Channel. It was originally launched as a way for fans of anime and other subculture topics in Japan to engage with each other. 4chan essentially just made an English version of 2chan and called it original. Further to this point, in 2015, 4chan was purchased by Hiroyuki Nishimura, a Japanese national who was an original administrator of 2chan. Thus, the snake has eaten its own tail.

TWO: Although people often think of 4chan for memes and even Engrish, Engrish.com came into being in 1996, seven years before 4chan was created. It was originally the personal blog of Steve Caires, an American expat living in Tokyo. He would take photos of all the defective English he encountered on his adventures and post them to his personal blog starting in 1996, which then took on the domain Engrish.com in 1999.[2]

THREE: And my final point, as a person living in Japan, you walk around and are just continuously confronted with random phrases or depictions that cause you to bust out laughing.[3] There

---

[2] Engrish.com is still quite active to this day, and if you want to get an even deeper sense of the ongoing daily hilarity, you should visit Engrish.com, because everyone needs to be told "Don't Tooth!" or to take a visit to the "Freak's Store". Not all these English missteps are Japanese. The Chinese are also a popular purveyor of quality Engrish. One of my personal favorites is a sign in Taiwan that reads "A wild dog haunts. Take care of yourself." I mean, how is that not 100x better than "Beware of stray dogs." and you better believe that if I'm ever in Taiwan, I'm finding that sign and taking a picture in front of it. Maybe I should just put one up on my gate to my backyard to confuse my pool guy.

[3] The complex pictograms are hilarious as well. David Sedaris titled his book <u>When You Are Engulfed in Flames</u> after a pictogram commonly found on smoking stations around Tokyo. When I read the title of the book, which came out a couple of years after my own experience, I immediately recognized the exact pictogram to which he was referring. It was a little drawing of a stick figure man running away holding his head, which was completely on fire. Next to him stood another stick figure holding a cigarette. Only a city as crowded as Tokyo would require people to smoke standing at stations to avoid lighting other commuters on fire. The stations were oblong metal basins with fans over them that could accommodate six or more people standing around them. The amazing thing about these contraptions was that people in fact used them. On any given day, I would walk by one or more smoking stations crowded with people blowing smoke into the vent and holding their cigarettes to the metal basin to avoid lighting each other and passersby on fire.

isn't any type of intention to go viral. There isn't even an intention for English speakers to see what they write. The Japanese, in particular, enjoy using English as a decoration on clothes and on signs. Occasionally, they do put it there for instructive purposes, but again, the intent is not to amuse English speakers. The little boy with the shirt covered in "fuck" was wearing that shirt because his mom thought it was cute, and if she knew what the word fuck meant in English, she didn't care enough to be embarrassed about it. In every sense, she had zero fucks to give that her son was walking around giving everyone who saw his shirt a whole lot of fucks.

In conclusion, everyone loves memes. I personally ingest a particularly unhealthy number of them every day, and the few people that are on the receiving end of my daily deluge probably regret signing up for Instagram or at least inviting me into their DMs. It is my highly unprofessional and barely researched opinion that we have the Japanese people's zero fucks about dunking on the English language to thank for the rampant meme culture that has made modern life worth living. You can deliver my Pulitzer Prize to Steve Caires.

So, Alia, what does this opus on the history of memes have to do with skull-fucking? Well, I would think it's obvious. As I wandered around Tokyo for five months, I encountered many quality examples of Engrish. From the "Happy Nuts Fair" advertisements of the Doutor coffee shop to the "Devil Robots" section of Kiddyland, a massive multi-floor toy store that offered all manner of questionably appropriate toys, there was a lot of Engrish to be found in my daily life. One particularly amusing sign popped up near my school. I was walking from Asakusa station to class one day

---

The pictograms referenced by Sedaris would be liberally pasted on these stations as consumer warnings.

when I spotted what is colloquially referred to as a gate. By gate, the Japanese mean something you walk through at the entrance of an establishment. In this case it was a cloth sign hanging in a doorway that read the following:

Sisimaru where you can enjoy selections from our wonderful Japanese men and up to the best sake.

I remember giggling uncontrollably when I first saw that gate. One day, when I was walking back to the station with my friend Mae, one of the Japanese students studying American law, I asked her if that place was a Host Club.[4] She looked at me like I had grown an extra head.

---

[4] A Host Club, or *Hotsuto Kurabu*, is an establishment where women go to seek the platonic but flirty company of young men. It's essentially the male version of a Hostess Club. Hostess Clubs, either *kyabakura* (a portmanteau but not direct translation of cabaret) or *kurabu* (club), are the modern take on the old school tea houses where *geisha* would entertain men by making conversation, lighting cigarettes, and pouring tea or sake for the men. Acting as a hostess is one of the traditional Japanese *geisha* skills, along with very specific dances and traditional musical instruments taught to *geisha* during their training. Modern days Hostess and Host Club employees forego the more skill-based duties and focus on pouring drinks, smiling, making polite conversation, and looking attractive. Hostess Clubs have been around for a long time, as you might imagine, but Host Clubs are a relatively new addition to the culture, the first one having been established in 1966. Host Clubs are generally a mirror image of a Hostess Clubs, except that often the hosts will do bits of comedy, magic tricks, or other forms of entertainment for the women. Also, the clientele varies greatly, with most Hostess Club tabs being paid by companies for the employees to entertain clients, and most Host Clubs catering to independent women. I did not visit either a Host Club or a Hostess Club while I was living in Tokyo, but I did visit a Maid Cafe (which is a story for another time). If you want to know more about the intricacies, many not so pleasant, of the Japanese Hostess Club culture before it was penalized and ultimately unionized in 2009, you might want to take a look

"That's just a restaurant," she said, overenunciating perhaps just enough that I felt she might have been evaluating me on my intelligence.

"But they are advertising their wonderful Japanese men," I replied, trying to keep my face straight.

By this point, I had already figured out the misunderstanding in translation, but her exasperation was too amusing. She rolled her eyes at me and walked on ahead. If you are confused, you are not alone. In Japanese, many words that are Romanized to include a "u" don't pronounce the trailing "u" when speaking. For example, the Japanese word for "is/am" is Romanized as d-e-s-u in the polite, present conjugation. However, d-e-s-u is pronounced "des." So, you can see how the word "menu" might end up as "men." This is a not uncommon outcome for English words ending with a "u" that are written by a Japanese-speaker.[5] So, a classy restaurant might put an English sign on their gate to add ambiance, not realizing that English speakers read the sign and make certain assumptions about the establishment based on a bit of frippery the restauranteur considers purely ornamental.

I encountered the single most offensive and hilarious bit of ornamental Engrish while shopping around in Ueno in late

---

at the Netflix documentary Missing: The Lucie Blackman Case, which delves into the systemic problems around the industry, particularly in the early 2000s, when many of the hostesses were *gaijin* working without a visa and thus easily exploited for fear of deportation.

[5] For instance, recently, I ordered some traditional *washi* from a Japanese factory named Awagami Factory that makes beautiful notebooks out of washi. They sent me a printed card expressing their thanks, and the last line read "Thank you once again from all of us here at Awagami......*Arigatou Gozaimas*. Once again, they Romanized a word without the trailing "u" at the end. We would write it *Arigatou Gozaimasu*.

January. I can't recall if it was in the store Magazines or Hinoya, but Ueno is known for its casual menswear shops and outdoor market, Ameyoko. Ginza might be high-end fashion, Harajuku might be trendy ladies' clothes, but Ueno was pseudo-American vintage menswear. I spent a chunk of time early in my stay wandering around that area, visiting the Ueno Science Museum, eating *takoyaki* (loosely fried dough balls with chunks of octopus inside) with my friend Becky in Ueno Park, and of course shopping.[6] I even recall my partner purchasing an oversized wool-cashmere blend great coat like something a salary man would wear from a stall in Ameyoko when they were visiting in February. It didn't have much utility in Florida and was ultimately donated, but it was like getting to play dress up in the weirdest way. In fact, by the time we all left Tokyo in May, a lot of the guys in my class had adopted this "American style" that Japanese men wore. I recall a guy in my class, Nick, was particularly into it, owning multiple t-shirts. One was a neon pink and orange monstrosity with a portrait

---

[6] This attempt at *takoyaki* eating was to the uproarious amusement of the Tokyo locals. In Ueno Park, the *takoyaki* is served in a paper tray like you would get for nachos at a baseball game. It comes with tiny skewers for utensils used to lance the balls and eat them. We couldn't get the doughy balls to stay on our glorified toothpicks, since they kept squirming off and falling or drooping precariously, as the dough was loosely cooked. It was a cold January day, and between the cold and our laughter, Becky and I could barely keep the toothpicks steady. A group of Japanese people at a nearby sitting area couldn't keep their shit together either. They busted out laughing at us, which only made us laugh harder. I yelled an apology to them in Japanese, and that just made it funnier. There is a very special feeling that you get when you make a Japanese person laugh at you in public, because you know how funny you had to be to incite it. Your utter ridiculousness is completely subsumed by the fact that you have incited genuine and uncontrollable joy in a stranger.

of I think Elvis Presley's face. I actually really loved those non-American-American shirts he would proudly sport.

On this particular day, I was wandering through the shops in Ueno, and I went into one of them that was touting its specialty as "vintage American." Dark wood paneling and open space reminded me of an Abercrombie store, but the contents were pure Japanese. I didn't realize it at the time, but when the Japanese say vintage American, they mean a style that resembled something you'd find in an American thrift store, not necessarily (although, sometimes, yes) actual clothes imported from America and resold. Wandering the racks of dark wash jeans and shirts, I came across a baseball-style 3/4 sleeve shirt with black, raglan sleeves.

On the front printed in black with a heavy glitter overlay was the word "I", followed by a skull and cross bones appliqued in black satin with gold embroidery over one eye hole, and the word "fuck" on the next line.[7] I did a double take. In what universe did the Japanese think the average American man would walk around with a shirt that said "I skull fuck" in glitter and satin with gold embroidery all over it? I mean, if we give the shirt designers the benefit of the doubt and assume they intended to say "I pirate fuck," I still think the glitter and satin would have precluded any adoption by American dude bros. After my shock wore off, I had a long, loud laugh and took a photo of the shirt design to show every person I ever had or ever would meet in my entire life.

Apart from the fact that this shirt was massively overpriced, I have no idea why I didn't purchase it. I should have yelled, "Take my money," and thrown my yen at the cashier like they do on TV shows! If there was any place in this entire wide world of seven

---

[7] If you look at the Ainote immediately before this story, you will see an ink and watercolor rendering of the shirt.

billion people that I could have walked around with such an atrocity on my chest and not gotten flack for it, it would have been Japan. I could have worn that shirt for five months in complete and utter anonymity (except maybe not to class), and brought it home as a souvenir, the kind you keep for the rest of your life and pull out when you're drunk and obnoxious. I could have it framed on the wall of my home office, offending anyone who dared to enter. I could wear it to The Castle in Tampa, which I haven't been to in at least two decades. I could be showing it to my great nieces and nephews in 30 years and regaling them of how their bad-ass grantie used to wear it around in a foreign country.[8] It is these little lost opportunities that we mildly regret for the rest of our lives, but the picture, at least, will live on.

---

[8] Our family uses grantie as a colloquialism for "great aunt."

AINOTE

I made this ink and watercolor sketch of a photograph that I took from the roof of the Mitaka no Mori Jiburi Bijutsu-kan (the Ghibli Museum) in Mitaka, Japan on a snowy winter day in February, 2008.

The museum building was designed by Hayao Miyazaki, one of the greatest animated filmmakers of all time and director of Studio Ghibli, to give visitors the ability to meander through the structure in different directions and elevations, capturing the spirit of the films. I was not allowed to take photos inside, so you will have to visit for yourself to see what wonders it holds. I have heard that it has been expanded since I visited and would love to get back there and see how it's evolved over the intervening years.

Supercilious!
How many can you think of?
Acrimonious!

Fuzzy, fluffy love—
wet nose buried in my arm.
Furry grin for days.

And the yarn dances,
melodic in its swirling—
order emerging.

Baby fingers curl.
Dark blue eyes blink and narrow.
A peal breaks the calm.

The dog eats paper.
She chews through thoughts on the page,
poetry and prose.

Pitter pat pat—
uneven gait reminds me
that my love grows old.

Knit purl knit purl knit—
covering my heart in wool,
shielded in softness.

KANAMARA MATSURI: THE FESTIVAL OF THE STEEL PHALLUS

The town of Kawasaki may make you think about the design and fabrication of crotch rockets, but a trip to Kawasaki in spring makes it evident that motorcycles aren't the only metal phalluses appreciated by the Japanese.[1] Kawasaki is home to the annual

---

[1] In truth, the city of Kawasaki has nothing to do with Kawasaki Heavy Industries, which was historically headquartered in both Kobe and Tokyo. Kawasaki the company is named after its founder, Shouzou Kawasaki and was one of three giant Japanese industrial *zaibatsu* (mega conglomerates), along with Mitsubishi Heavy Industries and Ishikawajima-Harima Heavy Industries. Nowadays, Kawasaki the company is part of the DKB Group, a *keiretsu*, or what might be considered a modern *zaibatsu* organization. Kawasaki the city does not appear to have any connection to Kawasaki the company. It is the second largest city in the Kanagawa prefecture, which lies south of Tokyo, the largest city being Yokohama. Kawasaki serves as a major connector between Yokohama and Tokyo. Although Kawasaki the city isn't related to Kawasaki the company, it is actually associated with heavy industry and technology through the companies JFE Group, Nippon Oil, Fujitsu, NEC, Toshiba, and others. Kawasaki has a population of over 1.5 million people and has the distinction of being the only city in Japan that is both over

Shinto festival, Kanamara Matsuri, or The Festival of the Steel Phallus. The phallus in question is a thick iron rod mounted pointing straight upward on top of a blacksmith's anvil. If you're wondering how I came to know of a Shinto festival worshipping a steel phallus, I can say that I had not heard of it in advance. My sister, who was visiting at the time from the United States, is pretty sure we learned about Kanamara Matsuri from one of my classmates. Either Kaoru or Becca seems like a good possible candidate for the suggestion, but I honestly have no recollection. She had just gotten out of the Peace Corps in February and so had been living in rural Uganda for the last year. Considering that this life had not exactly been swimming in technology and she had needed to take a substantial walk to Lugazi (population 110,000) to visit an Internet cafe to use the Internet to email or call my mom, she was determined to enjoy every last minute of the high tech insanity and casual hedonism that Japan provided.[2] It just so happened that she timed her arrival to be around my birthday, which is both right around *hanami* (cherry blossom viewing season), usually in early April, and Kanamara Matsuri, which takes place the first Sunday in April.

As I've previously mentioned, Japan has a complex relationship with sex, representations of sex in media, and what is and is not considered morally appropriate. In certain respects, the Japanese are much more open than we are in the United States. For instance, in 2008, when I would walk into a Don Quijote (pronounced Don Quixote or Donki for short in Japanese) in the

---

1 million in population but not a prefectural capital. Nevertheless, it thrives and every year attracts even more people to Kanayama Shrine for Kanamara Matsuri!

[2] See "Roppongi Redux," for more about adventures with my sister.

middle of Tokyo, I would find adult sex toys in the same aisle as the children's toys.[3] They are all toys, after all. Likewise, I would also find questionable material, such as the blood-spattered Gloomy Bear—I think there was even a plushy Gloomy biting the head off a little kid—for sale at Kiddyland, a multi-floor store in Ometesando dedicated to toys and characters (Star Wars, Hello Kitty, etc.), much of which was aimed at children. Just like other aspects of Japanese culture, Kanamara Matsuri had blurred lines.

Kanamara Matsuri was filled with penises of every size and material, but it was also a family festival. Penis-adorned red flags lining the sidewalk leading up to the shrine, penises carved of wood available for purchase, penis lollipops or ones shaped like little vulvas in every size and color, tiny wooden prayer boards with happy, cartoon penises etched on them, large wooden penises, complete with head, set up like cannons as a photo opportunity for people to ride on, a giant pink penis *mikoshi* (portable shrine—a sacred religious palanquin for Shinto practitioners), and of course the steel phallus itself, were just some of the ample penis paraphernalia provided to entertain the crowd of festivalgoers. Some of it was commercial, and some of it was religious, but all of it was open to the public, and there were many attendees of all ages. At the same festival, I saw both a little girl of probably four playing with and sitting on the steel phallus itself, and a man in his twenties was wearing nothing but strappy kitten heels and a short, silky kimono barely covering his butt that I'm 100% sure I saw for sale on the top floor of M's Pop Life Adult Department Store.[4]

---

[3] Essentially the Japanese equivalent of a War-Mart or Target for Americans or a Tesco for UK folks.

[4] I never knew the name of this store in Akihabara when I lived in Tokyo, since Google Maps didn't exist and I don't think the sign was in

Ron DeSantis's head might explode if one of his aides ever shows him this, but nothing about Kanamara Matsuri raises any eyebrows in Japan. No one is accused of sexualizing children because they are exposed to depictions of male genitalia during a fertility festival. Amazingly enough, a normal part of human anatomy that roughly 50% of the world's population possesses and which is required as one half of the creation of new life is, in fact, treated as a normal thing. Hell, the David isn't even depicted with an erection, and some American parents are still terrified that their child might actually see a stone penis. Forget a steel phallus, wooden erection, or the Elizabeth Mikoshi, the most garish of the *mikoshi* at Kanamara Matsuri, each of which is loud and proud with respect to the function of a penis.

Kanamara Matsuri got its start in 1969 and is held at the Kanayama Shrine, which is dedicated to Kanayama-*hiko* (a god) and Kanayama-*hime* (a goddess), which represent both metalsmithing, as well easy childbirth and protection from sexually transmitted diseases. In a way, blacksmithing and fertility might seem like a complete non sequitur, but it makes sense if you think about how the physical aspects of metalsmithing represent creating strong and useful tools, and fertility and protection from disease can be looked at as a metaphorical extension of that strength in protecting the body and helping it stay strong. Plus, there's the

---

English fifteen years ago, but its name is M's Pop Life, and it's supposedly the largest sex store in the world. I can verify that was in fact seven floors of adult paraphernalia. The first two levels were adult videos, followed by masturbatory aids (like vulvas in a can and stuff like that), then toys, then BDSM gear, lubes and such, lingerie, and finally costumes on the top level. It generally got tamer the higher you went and filthier the lower. It was most assuredly an entertaining place to visit, so if you are in Akihabara, it's worth checking out!

whole demon-possessed vagina thing. No, really! The original phallus mounted on the anvil is based on a story dating back to the Edo Period (1603-1868). Although the shrine was historically prayed at by blacksmiths, a legend sprung up during the Edo Period that centered on a demon that fell in love with a human woman. She, however, had the audacity to get married to a human man instead of reciprocating his affections, so the demon decided to inhabit and take over her vagina and use its sharp teeth to dismember the woman's husband's penis when they tried to get it on. Apparently, this woman had two husbands that lost their penises to this demon, although I'm not sure how she convinced the second guy to marry her once word got around about her cursed lady bits. Apparently, it was only after the second husband lost his member that the woman consulted a Shinto priest, and his solution was to have a blacksmith forge a metal dildo that she could use to break the teeth of the demon and drive him away. This particularly miraculous phallus, which while not *mikoshi*-sized is much too large for any human woman (who hasn't trained for such an act) to accommodate, is the one mounted on the anvil and considered the great treasure at Kanayama. Since there hasn't been a need to exorcise demon vaginas in centuries, the steel phallus has become an artifact over which to pray for protection against STDs.

Over the years, Kanamara Matsuri has grown into a large festival that brings a lot of tourism to Kawasaki, and the proceeds are used to fund HIV/AIDs research. Even in 2008, it was quite large. Back then, there was a *mikoshi* parade that went from the shrine and around the streets and back. We didn't arrive for the beginning of the festival, so it's possible the *mikoshi* had already been paraded through the streets before proceeding into the shrine courtyard. When we arrived, they were already moved into position in front of the shrine. Nowadays, I believe that the festival has grown so large that the parade at noon takes the *mikoshi* to a nearby park, and they stay there the whole day until the end of the festival in the afternoon. When we participated, the entire festival fit inside the grounds of the shrine, although it was packed with folks of all ages and nationalities.

There are three primary *mikoshi* that participate in Kanamara Matsuri. The oldest is the Kankiiamara Mikoshi, which is a simple square base and roof with a wooden phallus inside it. The Kanamara Boat Mikoshi is like an upgraded version of the Kankiiamara Mikoshi, with a fancy wooden boat-shaped base and pitched roof. It houses a large black iron phallus, and this *mikoshi* was actually donated by Hitachi Zosen.[5] The last of the three *mikoshi* is the Elizabeth Mikoshi, which is a giant pink dildo on a base with no roof over it. It is the longest and most visible of the three *mikoshi* and was donated by the Elizabeth Kaikan, which is a cross-dressing club in the Asakusabashi district of Tokyo. It is the least dignified but also the most fun, which is I guess how a lot of things go. Again, a majority of the legislators in Florida would keel over reading this. Maybe I should send them a copy?

All the *mikoshi* except the Elizabeth Mikoshi were tended by *miko* (temple maidens) of the Shinto shrine dressed in white robes

---

[5] Hitachi Zosen is not actually part of the Hitachi *kiretsu*, although it used to be. So, you may recognize the name Hitachi, because as a *kiretsu*, there were a lot of businesses operating under that name. Ironically, Hitachi does make a muscle massaging device called the magic wand, which is preferred by many people as their vibrator of choice. Despite the connection of the name, Hitachi Zosen is an engineering firm that specializes in heavy equipment and industrial metals. So, it would make sense that they would support this shrine for luck. The Hitachi vibrator connection is just a fun coincidence. The reason their *mikoshi* has a boat base is because they used to be shipbuilders, but that line of business has since been divested.

over red *hakama* (wide pants that are more like a split skirt) with head pieces that had tiny *shide* (white, zig-zagged streamers made of paper) hanging from them. Larger *shide* also adorned the shafts of the phalluses of each *mikoshi* as well. There was also a priestess dressed in a bright purple kimono with a hammered brass head piece carrying a scroll tied all over with colorful cords who presided over the ceremony.[6] It is the custom that each shrine is tended by a priest, not a priestess, but Kanamara broke tradition by having a priestess rather than a priest. The ceremony itself was conducted in Japanese with gravity but not formality. It was a celebration, after all.

After the solemnity of the ceremony was concluded, all the festivalgoers, us included, resumed our boisterous enjoyment of all things phallic. I personally grabbed some lollipops of varying sizes, rode the giant wooden penis cannons (with pictures to prove it), and did a lot of people-gazing, at both Japanese and *gaijin* alike. Lynette got a photo in front of the Elizabeth Mikoshi, alone, which seems like an impossibility nowadays. We also peeked at some of the fertility prayers left on the shrine, most written in Japanese, each inscribed on a little wooden tag with a jaunty penis or a baby emerging from a fruit on it, with a red string for hanging. It felt a little like praying, but the prayers are hanging from little hooks all throughout the shrine. The festival has grown so much that when I look at photos of it now, I'm so glad I was able to experience it back before the human crush made it impossible to enjoy fully. I guess the whole world likes a little bit of dick now and then!

---

[6] Purple kimono when worn by a priest indicate a high rank within the Shinto order.

AINOTE

I made this ink and watercolor of a photograph that I took of one of the oni (demons) guarding the entrance to Toda-ji (the "Great Eastern Temple") in Nara, Japan. The "Great Buddha Hall" where this oni is located is the largest wooden building in the world and a UNESCO World Heritage Site. It is home to the largest Buddha Vairocana statue. The original photograph was taken March 11, 2008. This particular oni is holding a calligraphy brush and a scroll, which is why he resonated with me.

A new thing sparkles
on the edge of my vision—
uncertain but keen.

When we grope about—
blind but hopeful, connecting
in the friendly dark.

I don't love you yet,
but the potential is there
for you to break me.

I lock my heart up
to protect it from danger,
but I'm the danger.

Beneath cherry trees,
we talk in quiet voices
of tomorrows dreams.

A single moment—
and time passes so slowly
when you are not here.

ROPPONGI REDUX

Now might a good time to tell you about the transcendentally awesome drag show that my sister and I saw together in Roppongi. I started this as a footnote but determined that it needed its own place in this book and deserved greater attention from you than can be provided by an aside. As you should know by this point in your reading, I was not a big fan of Roppongi for multiple reasons. Yakuza ties, sketchy bouncers who kept trying to muscle me into bars, and this lingering sense of desperation and exploitation that seemed to cling to the people I passed all contributed to my unease every time I made my way there.

However, my sister was adamant that we needed to go to one of two drag shows that she found in the Lonely Planet guide. She didn't care which one, but she wanted to go to one of them. At the time, with rudimentary online maps and winging it as the primary mode of finding places, I settled on the one that was at least in an area of Tokyo I was familiar with and was not that far away, which of course, turned out to be in Roppongi. The show's name is Roppongi Kingyo, although I had to look it up to remember this fact. It is apparently even more spectacular now, which I owe to the popularization of family-friendly[1] and artistic activities in Roppongi and the reduction of illegal and unsavory activities over time.[2] Back in 2008, Roppongi Kingyo was a fairly new show, perhaps only a few years old. The entrance to the establishment now sports a bright red door with many lights around it pointing the way to Roppongi Kingyo, but in 2008, despite it being only a short walk from the train station, my sister and I couldn't even find it on the first attempt.

Please remember that at this time, there was no Google Maps, and there were no smartphones other than the original iPhone which did not work in Japan. So, I had to look up how to get there from my home computer and then we had to somehow navigate there on our own with no GPS to guide us. Despite the fact that it was fairly easy to get around Japan, particularly Tokyo, even then, Roppongi Kingyo was not well-marked. So, the first time we made a plan to see Roppongi Kingyo, I eventually gave up in frustration after not being able to find the entrance. We had stalked back and forth along the road it was supposed to be on looking for any sign of this illusive establishment, and I was beginning to feel uncomfortable, since I knew we were likely drawing attention. I

---

[1] If you think a drag show isn't family-friendly, please go back and re-read "Kanamara Matsuri: The Festival of the Steel Phallus" to refresh on the Japanese litmus for morality.

[2] If you are someone who considers drag performances to be unsavory and think they should be illegal, you probably aren't reading this book. If you are, I apologize for the fact that you somehow managed to stumble your way into reading a book written by a person who supports gay, trans, and human rights. I'm sure you can return it. Better yet, buy a few more copies and have a burning party. My wallet won't complain. I might even make a donation to The Trevor Project or the National Center for Transgender Equality in your name!

dragged us home instead of continuing the search. My sister was super bummed out, but I promised her we'd try again. The drag show was one of a few activities that she absolutely, definitely wanted to see. Given that, we made a second attempt a couple nights later, and it was well worth the trouble. It ended up being down a side street and marked with a tiny red sign that we must have walked back and forth past multiple times on our first foray into Roppongi.

I have been to drag shows in the United States, and in my limited experience, the ones I have attended were boisterous celebrations of individuality, sometimes self-mocking, often funny, and fabulous in their costuming and attitudes. They are entertainment and a celebration and a reminder to straight, cis people that they are there and not to be ignored. Roppongi Kingyo is straight up art. I do not in any way say this to denigrate American drag shows. I am sure that there are some in the U.S. with the production value that Roppongi Kingyo brings to its audience, but this show was next level, both literally because the stage was moving all over the place and metaphorically, because I'm pretty sure my mouth was hanging open the entire time. The ladies of Roppongi Kingyo were not just there to entertain, raise awareness, or solicit laughs. They wanted our admiration, our wonder, and even some tears.

As we entered the building, we went through a doorway to a staircase that led down into a reception area with a check-in desk. At the time, the price of the show included a drink and a snack. We didn't have to drink the drink, but we had to buy the drink. I honestly can't remember what it costs to see the show, but I remember it felt expensive at the time. I know they've changed things since then, and now it seems as if it's a *nomihodai* (all you can drink) situation with food. At the time, my sister and I were shown to our seats which were side-by-side along a counter-height bar facing the stage. There were multi-levels to the seating area, and I could see tables below us with couples whispering to each other, small groups of salarymen drinking, and even families seated together, one which was celebrating the anniversary of an older couple. At least, that's what it looked like. There were balloons and cake.

Before the show began, I had the occasion to use the ladies' room and remember seeing posters in the stalls advertising the star performer. She didn't look like a drag queen at all. She looked like a diva you'd see in Las Vegas headlining at a major hotel center stage. I was sure that she wasn't just a drag queen but a trans woman at least mid-transition. Tucking is doable for everyone, but her breasts, which were barely covered, were as believable as mine. The delicacy of her costume and striking beauty was mesmerizing. I remember going back to our bar seats and whispering to my sister that these were ladies weren't just drag queens. And they really weren't.

The show is currently marketed as a neo-kabuki style of Japanese culture with a performance by a mix of men, women, and trans women showcasing theatrical performances. In our time, the show consisted of a series of energetic songs all highly choreographed to take advantage of numerous costume changes and a stage comprised of cubes on a grid that moved up and down to different heights as the performers danced and lip synced. I don't remember any actual men being on the stage, but honestly, I'm not sure if I would have been able to tell. What I could tell was that it was a cabaret that ranged from frilly and fantastical to hard and burlesque, and it held our attention for every moment. If I blinked too long, I missed some intricacy of costume change or stage movement. It was not just a change in costume or a change in stage, however. There was a fluidity of being that I appreciated. My expectations for genders and their roles were flipped upside down and challenged, even for someone with nothing but respect for the transgender experience.

One thing I noticed living in Japan in 2008 is that men in Japan get to dictate what is considered feminine and what is considered masculine. To a certain extent, that happens in the United States as well, but American categorization of femininity appears almost as a reactionary inverse to how Japanese men handle things. For example, in the United States, women might like pink, whether that was originally forced on them by societal expectations or not. American men, driven by toxic masculinity or male fragility might then reject pink as "girly". The men here might reject something as being too feminine, whereas in Japan, that thing might be a sign of female sexuality and is thus adopted by men. For example, you will see a lot of men in Japan with pink cell phones, because pink symbolizes sexuality and arousal as it relates to women. So, men will embrace and adopt that symbolism and thus control it in a way that seems completely counter to how men in the United States might treat that same object.

This analysis is entirely based on stereotypical behavior, so I understand that there are many nuances not addressed here, and I appreciate that you, the reader, might be complaining to yourself how I've oversimplified a complex situation or otherwise lumped every man (whether American or Japanese) into one category of maleness. Trust that I do understand that this situation is a lot more nuanced than this explanation allows for. My goal here is to highlight how Japanese men, sometimes, might embrace femininity as way to assert power in exactly the same way that American men might reject femininity to assert power. All this is to say that transitioning to female in Japan, while similar in the loss of male privilege and those various other issues that present themselves to trans women in the United States, has a certain complexity to it due to the fact that the power of men in Japan isn't just in rejecting femininity but also in the taking of that femininity for oneself.

I am not a gender studies professor, and I certainly don't have any research about gender in Japan to back up my opinions, so I can only tell you what I've observed living in both cultures. According to my observations, there is a certain flexibility of thought that comes with exercising femininity in Japan that perhaps is less dimensional in the United States. That, of course, raises other questions. Perhaps the same issue of truly being seen as a woman still exists for Japanese trans women. Instead of being seen by men as a man who rejected the privilege of being a man, as is the case in the United States by those that refuse to accept that gender is separate from sex, they are still seen as men but men who have used their power to adapt female characteristics. In the end, it may still feel as if their authentic self isn't being truly appreciated, but it certainly appeared, in 2008, to be better tolerated as a legitimate expression than it was (and continues to be) in the United States.

AINOTE

I made this ink and watercolor of a photograph that I took of Shinkyo bridge, which serves as the entrance to Nikkō, Japan.

Sunday sinks the boat,
once riding the waves body—
now broken adrift.

Anhinga feathers
spread wide to the open air—
a successful hunt.

Scattering like leaves,
thoughts blow in the wind—rustling,
branches bent away.

Pull a gentle thread,
then walk away in the dark—
a sad melody.

Light, color, sound, movement
fades away to the background,
only an embrace.

Cold fingers, warm skin—
goose flesh rises like a wave,
crashed against the shore.

Your scent on my sheets,
memory softly clings like
your voice in my ear.

ALL GOOD THINGS MUST COME TO AN END...

Except perhaps Ise Jingu Shrine, which gets rebuilt from scratch every twenty years.

It's always tough to say goodbye. As I did the research to write this last story, in which I want to talk about the Shinto concept of *tokowaka* and the renewal process of Shikinen Sengū, I struggled to tie my disparate feelings into a pretty package—feelings towards Japan, towards my experience, towards beginnings and endings, and towards my growth as a person. It was as I was finally settling in to put these words to the page that I lost my stepfather. He was a steady presence in my life for twenty-nine years, and in the end, he declined rapidly from multiple illnesses directly stemming from Agent Orange exposure during the Vietnam War. It was not the ending I wanted for him or our relationship. It was traumatic and heartbreaking for my whole family. I paused with this project to process the grief of that loss, to think about the endings and beginnings that they create. Going through the grief experience once again, which last occurred in 2005 when I lost my grandfather, has reminded me that for me grief is the process of converting the trauma and pain of loss into an enduring set of memories that feed my heart when I feel low. I dust off all of those fantastic memories and set them on a shelf in my heart where I can be reminded of love, kindness, strength, and laughter. I rebuild that relationship and discard the trauma where it doesn't serve me and renew the spirit of the relationship. How does this relate to Ise Jingu?

The concept of *tokowaka* is a Shinto belief that to remain eternal and fresh, and to maintain divinity, an object needs to go through a regular process of renewal. The Jingu shrine in Ise is usually considered the embodiment of the concept of *tokowaka*. It may seem counterintuitive at first, but this renewal process, or Shikinen Sengū is conducted by completely destroying the sacred shrine and rebuilding it entirely in an alternate site from completely new materials. *How can something be considered eternal if it only exists for twenty years?* is a question I asked myself before I really began to dig into the concepts of Shinto. It turns out that in *tokowaka*, the idea is that we can preserve something in its spirit by being willing to completely change it, to make it young again. This serves multiple purposes for Shinto. The shrine itself is young and fresh and new, but also, it is eternal because it is rebuilt every twenty years during Shikinen Sengū, over a lengthy eight-year period, that uses the exact same processes and rituals that were used to build the original shrine over a thousand years ago. How to build the shrine is never forgotten. It becomes eternal in its spirit, in the action of continuously renewing it.

I'm by no means a religious or spiritual person, but I believe *tokowaka* has some applicability to me personally. I don't go out and get stem cell transplants every few years or anything like that. I do, however, revisit times in my life, like I'm doing now with this collection of stories, and I rebuild them in my mind, reconstruct them with additional context and try to keep them fresh and continuously applicable to how I live my life and grow as a person. Our personal histories, no matter how we try to reinvent ourselves will always to a certain extent inform who we evolve into as we age. You may have wonderful experiences, traumatic ones, mundane ones, or ones that shatter your sense of self for the better or worse. Most of us have a mix of these in varying allocations. Some of us get the short end of the stick with the wonderful experiences and end up with a heavy dose of trauma. It's not equal, and it's not fair, but it's always an opportunity to review, rebuild, and grow.

Is anything or anyone ever actually eternal? Even the universe has a projected end date, so probably not. But that doesn't mean we can't benefit from a little mental renewal every so often. So, although I can't say that my journey to Ise to see the Jingu Shrine held any real epiphany for me, I think if I hadn't stopped to learn about the concept of *tokowaka*, I would perhaps have lost out on an idea that has been beneficial for my larger emotional journey.[1]

If you're wondering why I failed to have that epiphany, I hate to be the bearer of bad news, but the Naiku and Geku inner sanctums aren't actually open to visitors. One of the last things I

---

[1] It is perhaps worth noting here that I was very surprised to learn while living in Japan that many of the castles and shrines that are known as heritage sites and culturally significant landmarks have burned and been repeatedly rebuilt over the centuries. As most traditional architecture in Japan is wooden, I guess this shouldn't have been as much of a surprise as it was, but the Japanese perhaps place less reverence to the structures themselves than on their design and ideas. The world watched in horror as Notre Dame burned almost exactly five years ago to the day this was written, and I can't help but think that this level of destruction has happened repeatedly to the Japanese people. In fact, just months after Notre Dame burned, Shuri Castle in Okinawa saw a similar fate. It had already been completely destroyed in 1945 and had only been fully restored since 1992. To learn more, see the following article: https://www.latimes.com/world-nation/story/2019-10-31/japan-historic-castle-fire.

did before I left to come home was to visit Ise as part of a trip to Kyoto and Nara. Be warned that if you make the pilgrimage there, you are unlikely to see anything that a tourist might consider worthwhile. The gate and a gravel walk up to it are the only access points. The alternate site can be looked at as well, as it remains unused unless you visit during the rebuilding period. But the Naiku and Geku themselves are closed off only to the priests and the imperial family. In fact, Princess Aiko, the only child of Emperor Naruhito, just made her first solo visit to Ise Jingu after her recent graduation from Gakushuin University, presumably to pray to Amaterasu. I have no bitterness that Japan hasn't opened its sacred sites to gawkers, but it is something worth understanding before you make the trip.

I didn't think too much about this concept of *tokowaka* when I was in Ise or when I returned to the United States shortly after, but it was seeded there and has spread tendrils gently over time. Like all endings, I grieved the closing of a monumental experience in my life, my first true immersion into another culture. Simultaneously, I was excited to return home to a country that wasn't a fourteen-hour time difference from every member of my immediate family, that had real pancakes,[2] and where no one would

---

[2] The only place in Tokyo where you could truly get an American breakfast in 2008 was Fujimamas, which was a restaurant owned by Americans. It was so popular in Tokyo that they opened a shop in Hawaii. You could get all sorts of actual American breakfast and lunch specialties in Harajuku, Tokyo. Japanese tend to think American breakfast food is way too sweet and often market it as desserts. One of my favorite *yoshoku* restaurants used to serve soft serve ice cream parfaits layered with chocolate syrup and corn flakes. Waffles and crepes were similarly decorated with toppings and eaten as desserts. My friend Amey and I found Fujimamas after I lamented my deep need for pancakes, butter, and maple syrup with eggs and bacon. Given that it was at least a thirty-minute trip by train and walking from my

stare at me as I went about my business or assume that I was lost, confused, or stupid just because I was looking at a map. I knew I would miss a lot of things about Japan (and continue to miss, let's be honest), including Choco-Cro, Mister Donut, apple tea, Moss Burger, Jonathan's, *tabehodai shabu-shabu*, crepe stands, *omurice*, *hanami* season, hot cocoa from vending machines on a January morning, cheap curry katsu stands stationed at every shrine, *nomihodai karaoke* rooms, all things yuzu, train travel (especially *shinkansen*), taking *onsen*, random Engrish everywhere, people living their lives in cosplay for no discernable reason, that salmon nigiri with the kewpie and micro-sliced onions, and a ton of other tiny details, food-related or otherwise. Sadly, I left before many modern Japanese offerings like cat cafes (and now corgi cafes and even capybara cafes exist), jiggly Japanese cheesecakes, and so much more that are currently packed into saved Instagram reels in anticipation of my next visit.

 It is the process of documenting these experiences, engaging in active renewal of old, cherished stories, memorializing the original spirit of the adventure into a fresh new creative outlet that has crystalized for me the true value of *tokowaka*. Maybe all acts of memoir are *tokowaka* in some respect. They aren't planned and executed with rigor like the craftsmanship required for the Jingu Shrine, fresh 1300 years after being first built, but as an act of renewing the spirit of me individually. As I enter yet another phase of my life, I'm truly grateful that I have such experiences to look back on, dust off, share with you, and ultimately grow from.

---

guesthouse, I didn't make it there super often, but just knowing pancakes were an option warmed my heart. It was lively, always did brisk business, and served both expats and Japanese alike. Sadly, around exactly a year after I left, it shuttered for good, ostensibly due to the rent almost doubling in Harajuku.

ACKNOWLEDGMENTS

In the most basic sense, this book would not be possible without the Beasley School of Law at Temple University, Japan Campus (TUJ) and its Dean and President, Matthew J. Wilson, J.D., who at the time of my attendance was a professor and the Dean of the law school, but who has since assumed leadership as the Dean and President of the entirety of TUJ. I knew that I would be attending TUJ before I had even selected a law school to attend, and Professor Wilson was key in not only welcoming me and the other students, but in providing a stellar experience academically, culturally, and practically. I would also like to thank my other professors and the TUJ support staff, including Stanley Yukevich, Edward Yeh, Gerald McAlinn, Jonathan C. Blaine, Min Lu, and Misako Hockersmith. Additionally, my fellow students, Carrie Nguyen, Rebecca Gross, Rebecca Grausam-Charamella, Olivia Pulley-Crowther, Erin Worrell, Jennifer Ryan, Kaoru Nakamura, Patrick Griffin, Allen Mendenhall, Paweł Wójcik, Nick Bono, CiJe Rabess, May Horimoto, April Williams-Shaw, Jhon Sanchez, Matthew Wendler, Evan Tarkington, Matt (Houston) Wiggington, Chad Reid, John Alan Kawai, and the others that made my adventure so particularly memorable, I continue to cherish the memories we share from Japan. Finally, among my TUJ community, I want to mention and acknowledge Carly Foreback, one of my classmates who we tragically lost to undiagnosed leukemia in 2019. She was such a kind and generous person, always ready for a laugh.

From those that helped form these stories at the time I lived them, I also want to thank Lynette Luria, Amey Lueck Krauser, and

Day Amberhart. Hosting my friends and family while I was abroad made all the difference, and I will never forget the times we had, good or bad.

Further, I want express my great appreciation to my FDU writing community, including Heather Lang-Cassera and Elizabeth Jaeger. Both of you were integral in ensuring that this project got completed, and I am so excited that we all have all been published with Unsolicited Press together as a cohort.

And finally, thank you so much to the team at Unsolicited Press for accepting my mixed media proposal and giving this collection a home. I am so proud to be published by such an amazing press.

ABOUT THE AUTHOR

Alia Luria at Kanawara Matsuri (Festival of the Steel Phallus) in Kawasaki, Japan, April 2008.

Alia Luria is a novelist and creative non-fiction writer living in Florida. Her debut science fiction novel, *Compendium*, won the National Indie Excellence Award in 2015 in the Fantasy category, the Reader's Favorite Silver Medal in Fantasy and was a finalist for the Independent Author Network Book of the Year Award in Fantasy, Science Fiction, and First Novel. Her second novel in the series, *Ocularum* will be published by Something or Other Publishing. Her essay "You Might Eat Organic, but You're Full of Baloney" was a creative non-fiction finalist for the Malahat Review Open Season Awards in 2018 and was ultimately published by the Northwest Review in the Winter 2021 edition. It has since been republished in the anthology *Women Write Now*, curated by Edna White.

Alia received her MFA from Fairleigh Dickinson University in 2018 in the fiction concentration. You can find Alia on Instagram as @alialuria and on Facebook. Her author website is alialuria.com and her blog is stillnotarobot.com. She also designs and publishes knitwear patterns as Crypto Knits, and you can view her designs at cryptoknits.com.

ABOUT THE PRESS

Unsolicited Press is based out of Portland, Oregon and focuses on the works of the unsung and underrepresented. As a womxn-owned, all-volunteer small publisher that doesn't worry about profits as much as championing exceptional literature, we have the privilege of partnering with authors skirting the fringes of the lit world. We've worked with emerging and award-winning authors such as Ay Shimshon-Santo, Heather Lang-Cassera, John W. Bateman, Douglas Cole, Elisa Carlsen, and Sung J. Woo.

Learn more at unsolicitedpress.com. Find us on instagram, X, bsky, threads, youtube, facebook, and pinterest.